Saudi Arabia

The Great Adventure

The Americans
Who Helped A Remote Desert Kingdom
Become One Of The Richest Nations
In The World

Introduction: Cassandra L. Oxley • Text & Photographs: Owen Oxley • Design: Alyssa A. Oxley

Saudi Arabia
The Great Adventure

Published by Stacey International
128 Kensington Church Street
London W8 4BH
Tel: 020 7221 7166 : Fax 020 7792 9288

Library of Congress Cataloging-in-Publication Data

Oxley, Owen
Saudi Arabia
The Great Adventure
The Americans Who Helped A Remote
Desert Kingdom Become One
Of The Richest Nations
In The World

ISBN 1905299 079

1. Middle East - 2. Arabian American Oil Company (Aramco) - 3. Kingdom of Saudi Arabia - 4. Photographs - 5. Essays

Book design by Alyssa Oxley. Design production by Ann DeCerbo, DeCerbo Design.

Copy edited by Maarten Reilingh.

Printing & Binding: SNP
Leefung, China

Dedication

To: Mary
       Laura
       Wanda
       Cassandra
       Alyssa
       Madeleine
       Eliza Jane
       Lorrie
       and
       Ben

Contents

Prince Mishaal, guest of honor at dedication of new power company, Al Khobar, in 1952.

Main street, Al Khobar.

(left) Children play before Great Fort, Hofuf.

Acknowledgements

New Aramco logo.

At different moments in the last fifty years I reached out in search of people who could help me with this book, hoping against hope that some of them might still be about and that, even more important, their memories were still clear and bright. I am happy to report that I was surprised at their numbers and even more delighted at their willingness to clearly recall certain events that occurred during the last half century and which I wished to refer to as accurately as possible. Inevitably—and fortunately—they were able to correct a number of mistaken impressions that I have lugged about in my head for years.

While I have read and written on Aramco and Saudi Arabia over these many years, the major impetus for The Great Adventure came about when I returned to Arabia in 1979 for a client. I knew that many amazing changes had taken place since I left in 1955, nearly a quarter century before. Not everything was to my liking, but the progress in so many small things and in several of the big ones was collectively very impressive. So, before I left for Arabia, I had determined that during the several weeks I would be in the field to look up as many of the people I knew in the fifties, as a beginning point.

I went to Jiddah and met with W. Jack Butler (and his

Man and beast.

wife, Pat) my boss for several years in Dhahran. He was now chairman of the board of Mobil Saudia, charged with building a brand new, 675-mile long pipeline from Jubail to Yenbo. He was very helpful to me and provided a crucially valuable perspective of certain aspects of the challenges faced by the public relations department in those early days. (See "Keeper of the Gates", beginning on page 26.) Later on, following his retirement, we met on several occasions in New York City, where he counseled me on the progress of the book.

Following my visit to Jiddah, I returned to Dhahran and sought out Saleh Soweyah, a member of Aramco's government relations department in the fifties, one of the first Saudis to achieve senior staff status. I learned that he had retired from Aramco and was now an agent for the Pillsbury Company, whose corporate headquarters were in Minneapolis, Minnesota, where I lived. His place of business was in Dammam, so I drove down and found him sitting in a large, attractive office. His operations

seemed to be very successful, considering the size of his facilities and all the people seeking his signature or peppering him with questions.

When he got over his surprise at seeing me, I asked about him and his family, expecting nothing more than a perfunctory response. However, he startled me by saying, "I should tell you that my first wife was barren, so I took a second one, who bore me two daughters." He looked at me and smiled.

"Well," I said, "In this enlightened day and age, what would you like to see them do, accomplish in life?"

He thought about this for a moment, "First of all, I hope they will be intelligent enough to be accepted by the University of Petroleum and Minerals." He paused, pursed his lips, and said, "If they are not, I will send them to America for their education." We both burst out laughing. Then we talked about the past.

I went back to Aramco's administration building in Dhahran and asked directions to the office of John Kelberer, then chairman of the board of Aramco, which I found on the second floor. I walked in, gave my name to his secretary, and asked to see him. "Please mention, if you would, I was here in 1950, and that I am from Minnesota." A moment later, I was ushered into his office.

He was very gracious. I explained that I was planning to write an article that would feature two executives who headed up Aramco at two of the most crucial points in the history of the company: Fred A. Davies and John Kelberer, both Minnesotans, both graduates of the University of Minnesota, one from St. Paul and the other from Winona. When finished, the piece would be submitted to the *Minneapolis Tribune*, a major daily newspaper. I said I couldn't guarantee its publication but thought it surely would appeal to a discerning editor.

As a minor but pertinent fragment of the story, I asked if he could provide me with the number of Minnesotans currently working for Aramco in the field, which I thought would be of interest to the *Tribune's* readers. He said to stop by in the next day or so for that count.

Finally, he said he was leaving shortly on vacation and gave me his home number. If I needed to talk to him, he'd be there in a couple of weeks upon my return to Minneapolis, I did call him and then wrote the piece—which also made reference to the 60 or so Minnesotans employed by Aramco. It was published many months later—August 13, 1990—on the Op-Ed page. Operation Desert Storm had already gotten underway. Mr. Kelberer's hopes that the situation could be resolved without bloodshed were of no avail.

The Arabian.

Some time ago, I combined a business trip to California with a visit to Thomas (Tommy) F. Walters, Aramco's chief public relations photographer with whom I worked. He had spent almost 14 years based in Dhahran, heading up by the time he retired a very large photographic department. He and I had a first-rate time recapitulating the past. Since then, I have called him many times with questions, most of which he was able to answer.

He permitted me to use several photographs that he had taken on two separate occasions, one in Bahrain, and the other while on assignment with an exploration crew, all duly credited. I also found Vern Tietgen, a writer with the department, living in The Dalles, Oregon. At 93 and in good health, he was very helpful at almost every step of the way. The pieces began to come together.

One of the most helpful people in this web of memories and manners was Ray T. Graham, who was in at the very beginning of the formation of CASOC, which is covered in "'Dry Holes' in Dammam" (page 22). I drove down to Rhode Island to interview Pat Metz, widow of Homer Metz. Pat regaled me with numerous hilarious, some downright outrageous tales about Homer, manager of public relations for Aramco and Tapline for more than a dozen years, principally in Beirut. In Salisbury, Connecticut, I located and interviewed Howard Beir who went out to Arabia in 1946 and pioneered the first-ever press relations function for Aramco (see page 26, "Keeper of the Gates"). He died January 23, 2005, at age 87.

Upon meeting his wife Amy (Ward), I recalled knowing her as having worked in Aramco's New York public relations department, then located at 505 Park Avenue. I was even more astonished when in casual conversation with her I learned that she was the daughter of Thomas E. Ward, who in 1926 negotiated the sale by the Eastern & General Syndicate Limited of certain concessions which eventually led to the several oil developments in Bahrain, Saudi Arabia, Kuwait, the Neutral Zone, and Quatar. A British citizen, he was the founder and president of Oilfield Equipment Company until his retirement in 1958.

He was instrumental in urging Major Frank Holmes, the intrepid New Zealander, to insinuate himself into the good graces of Ibn Sa'ud, then emir or sultan of Nejd, to sign a contract that would provide an exclusive option to the E&GS for the exploration of oil and other mining rights in the province. For various reasons, most particularly the fact that none of the oil companies approached felt any hope of discovering oil, the contract languished, much to the irritation of Ibn Sa'ud.

In August of 2004, I went down to Pinehurst, North Carolina, to attend the 24th Biennial Annuitants Reunion, where almost 500 former Aramcons gathered to visit, play tennis, golf, enjoy a libation or two, and reminisce about the past. I found only three people I knew back in the fifties, all of whom I was delighted to see and talk

to about their current lives, reliving moments from the past that provided the clarity I needed for stories I was writing. The overall spirit present was palpable, stunning in its sincerity and simplicity.

Since then, I have been sending pictures all over the country for other people to examine and to put names to faces. I sent a half dozen to Pete Speers who, unsure about a couple, send them on to Pete Goddard for confirmation. John Rufus Jones was drawn into the process at Pinehurst. He turned out to be a veritable warehouse of good stuff, and I have talked with him several times. I called Gip (and Virginia) Oldham, about aviation. Also at Pinehurst were Monique and Janny Slotboom from Holland. They steered me to William Chandler, former Tapline president, an incredible source with a superb memory. Also Ash Kearney, and his son, John. Bill Brown of Exploration, sent me a set of pictures taken by T.F. Walters. Former safety engineer Paul Pederson (with wife Claire) shed considerable light on one curious happening, which led to him clearing up another ticklish question I posed to him.

Falcon.

I also met Tim Barger, who has published several books on Saudi Arabia, particularly <u>Out in the Blue</u>, the collected letters (1937–40) of his father, Thomas C. Barger, a geologist, one of the first young men who explored the deserts of Arabia and eventually became president and CEO of Aramco. The book of letters to his wife Kathleen, is wonderfully factual, totally charming, and quite difficult to put down. Tim was very helpful to me to me when I met him at Pinehurst, and even more so since, providing a number of insights into the publishing business that have saved me both time and money. I had been talking to William Tracey for several years and finally met him at

Pinehurst for a couple of good, long chats. He used some of my pictures in a display several years ago.

From an entirely different and unexpected quarter, I received a telephone call from H. Clark Griswold, someone who lives just a few miles away from me (Woodbury, in Litchfield County, Connecticut), and who had seen an article making reference to the book. A banker for more than three decades in the Middle East for Chemical Bank of New York, Lehman Brothers, and others, he had

A lizard of the desert, nonpoisonous.

known a number of the more entrepreneurial Saudi Arabs, several of whom became extremely successful and wealthy through the combination of their own energies and initiatives—and the cooperation of Aramco.

One man in particular stood out in Clark's mind: Sulayman Olayan, for whom Clark eventually worked as vice president of his holding company (OICE). Olayan had been involved in the construction of the 1,067-mile long, 30–31 inch pipeline from Ras Tanura to Sidon, Lebanon. Clark made available to me a biography of Suliman Olayan, entitled From Unaizeh to Wall Street, authored by Michael Field, which was published in 2000, but received limited distribution.

I called Arthur Clark, editor of Al~Ayaam Al~Jamilah, for some information, and learned that he had just been given my name as the source for some pictures. This led to my writing an article, "In Search of a Portrait," for his book, which was received quite well by its readers. He has been extremely helpful to me in so many ways that I simply can't list them all. David D. Bosch, of the Washington, D.C., office of Aramco Services Company, was instrumental in checking facts and text as well as securing a picture needed to complete a story in The Great Adventure.

There are many more, too many to mention, but I must especially thank Ms. Yvonne Loo who I met at Pinehurst. When chatting with her, I referred to Discovery, by Wallace Stegner, as a book I was looking for; she went directly to her room and returned with a copy, which she insisted on giving to me. And Ms. Mary Lorray who came to see me at the Souk to talk about Ras Al Mishaab. Together we explored a subject that yielded no answers then, and may never. It's something that we will both ponder for a long time.

A last minute phone/fax exchange with Mike Ameen was extremely valuable in identifying several members of the royal family.

Finally, I want to thank my daughter, Cassandra, for her introductory piece, which nicely captures the context of the last fifty years, and for my other daughter, Alyssa, for establishing the striking graphic format for the book, which Ann DeCerbo of DeCerbo Design, Norfolk, Connecticut, has beautifully carried through to make a handsome and memorable measure of those extraordinary times. I also owe a considerable debt of gratitude to John Ammaturo, whose varied interests in the petroleum, construction, and publishing industries, encouraged me to proceed.

A major regret of mine is that I have been unable to put a name to every face and a date to every picture in the book. Accordingly, I have decided that upon publication I will produce a separate insert that will contain as many names and dates as possible, keyed to specific pages in the book.

If you are able to identify someone not identified, please inform me via e-mail at: oxo@bestweb.net. This will enable me to assemble the insert, which I will then send to everyone who provides me with an address. If the book goes into a second printing, I will also add the name(s) wherever appropriate in the book. Thank you.

The basic donkey.

Why This Book?

W ell, one reason is that most photographers take pictures on the assumption that they will be used at some point, in one agreeable format or another. The sooner the better, of course. A half-century is a tad long, I'll admit.

A further hope is that they will be appreciated by a photo-editor, cropped appropriately, and be of a size that does justice not only to the subject but to the inherent value of the picture. If reproduced in a publication of quality or distinction, so much the better. If a credit line correctly identifies the photographer, even better still. A state of near-Nirvana will have been achieved. It's ego-related, I'm told.

All of the pictures in this book were taken more than fifty years ago, many of them unpublished, unseen. They represent duplicates, outright rejects, and cover a few subjects considered irrelevant or sensitive at the time taken. The pictures speak for themselves, covering as they do almost every segment of the operations of the Arabian American Oil Company (Aramco) during the first extraordinary burst of growth and expansion following World War II.

The coverage of the Saudi government, the royal family, the town Arab, and especially the Bedouin, is fragmentary and highly selective, as might be expected. It wasn't quite the age when sketching, painting, or taking a photograph of someone was tantamount to stealing the subject's soul, but at a few of the more remote locations there were indications of apprehension—a frown, a warning wave of the hand, or a turning away from the camera. Discretion and good judgement were always important elements in the documentary process.

I went where I was sent. (Not everywhere—it was to be another 24 years before I got to Jiddah.) On arrival, I photographed what was required, what I saw. Just how to classify these pictures today is a bit of a puzzle. They are certainly documentary. Perhaps they are photo-journalism (ala Life magazine). Or they are pure and simple publicity pictures, the assignments carried out to promote the many aspects of a brand-new oil company's operations in an age-old land. Some day they might even be considered archival. Wow!

A s for the essays and articles that accompany several of the picture spreads, they were written based on notes made a short while after a particular event or assignment. I have written about what I saw and experienced without exaggeration or varnish. They collectively represent the facts of the moment, as they were, as I saw them. Perhaps they tell more than the pictures.

These pictures and text are like no other book produced over the years by former Aramcons, all of which—almost without exception—are valuable in that each one provides a personal perspective on experiences and accomplishments unique to that individual or family.

I hope the pictures in this book—more than three-hundred of them—will remind the men, women, and children who worked, lived, and grew up in Saudi Arabia as members of the "Family of Aramco" of the unique role they played in helping a remote desert kingdom become one of the richest nations in the world. For once upon a time, very few people could tell you just where Saudi Arabia was on the world map.

T oday, Aramco as we once knew it, is no more. An embryonic oil company that for several generations did the bidding of its several owners (including Saudi Arabia), SaudiAramco is now a colossal energy giant owned and operated by the Kingdom of Saudi Arabia, its daily operations and actions minutely scrutinized by the rest of the world.

For me and for many others, it was a Great Adventure.

Al Humdilila!

December 10, 2005

Norfolk, Connecticut

C.L. Oxley

A Half Century

Cassandra L. Oxley

When my father asked me to write the introduction to this book, I was apprehensive, pointing out that I had been away from Arabia for such a long time that I would not be able to set the tone or perspective he might like. He assured me that I could do it, saying that I need not do a conventional intro but frame it within our family's experience in and continuing interest with Arabia over more than 50 years. But be sure to start at the beginning, he said. The very beginning.

I was born about mid-morning on January 21, 1955, a Friday, the holy day of Moslems. It took place at the new Dhahran Health Center, Dhahran, Saudi Arabia. My precise birth date and time of delivery was selected by Dr. R.C. Brown, a doctor at the Health Center. He had determined that as I had not turned correctly in the birth canal, a Cesarean section was called for. My father- and mother-to-be were quite nervous but, happily, all went well and mom and I went home a few days later to a delighted and much relieved father. I was named Cassandra Lea and weighed 8 lbs, 12 ozs. I prospered, put on weight, and was an entirely agreeable baby, from all I can gather.

In May of that same year, my father and mother (Owen and Wanda Oxley) left Arabia after a 30-month stay for a well-earned long vacation. This was the second tour completed by my family and my father was unsure whether he would return for another. He was asked to defer his decision until the end of the vacation, the thought being that at the end of a wonderful, expensive vacation he would be more than ready to return for another tour. However, he did resign, concluding almost six years

service with Aramco in New York and Arabia, in such departments as General Service, Accounting, Exploration, and Public Relations. For him, it had been a very happy and valuable experience. It was time to move on. Aramco, in due course, hired a new young photographer named E.E. Seal. Years later, he talked to my father and apparently expressed delight at finally talking to the man who had opened up such an exciting job opportunity for him!

Wanda Oxley, Rub Al Khali.

Virtually every aspect of that Middle East association had been rewarding, I gathered over the subsequent years, and my parents continued to follow with great interest the developments—good and bad—that were taking place in Saudi Arabia. For that matter, almost the entire Middle East appeared to be in a state of turmoil at some point or another, influenced by religion, politics, and nationalism. Oil was never far off center stage, with America drawn into more and more of these developments. Tumultuous times were in the offing everywhere,

it seemed, although our family's special focus was Saudi Arabia and Aramco.

In fact, a major crisis developed a few months before my parents got married on Bahrain Island (December 11, 1953). Mohammed Mossadegh, a powerful cleric (who in 1951 had nationalized the Anglo Iranian Oil Company and forced the shah to flee Iran) and at that time prime minister of Iran, was himself overthrown on August 19 and the shah of Iran restored to the throne. Mobs took to the streets of Teheran and other cities, with deaths and damage to oil facilities reported in the world's press. It was rumored the United States had played a major but covert role in this coup with the Central Intelligence Agency (CIA) very much a player. Nevertheless, Aramco remained aloof, unaffected, its employees seemingly undisturbed throughout these days.

Another momentous event was the long-expected death of Ibn Sa'ud, which occurred later that year, on November 9, 1953. The succession by his eldest son—Crown Prince Sa'ud—took place in an orderly fashion, testifying to the stability of the government. King Sa'ud soon toured Al Hasa Province, visiting Hofuf and Dhahran, and various tribes in the area, tranquility the order of the day. Aramcons went on doing their jobs, new wells were drilled, oil flowed, royalties mounted as never before.

But not for long, as Aramco was struck—it'd probably be called a work stoppage these days—by its employees in all three districts, with the organizers (some Saudis, as well as Palestinians, and others) listing grievances an

(left) At a remote desert location a new well comes in.

demanding concessions. It was all rather low-key with no real violence and little damage to plants or facilities, the Saudi police and army units relatively restrained in their handling of the matter. Together Riyadh, Hofuf, Jiddah, and Dhahran addressed the demands and resolved the legitimate ones. Within a few weeks, the strike was over. Little oil production was lost. This happened in June of 1955, barely a month after my parents had left the field.

By an odd coincidence, H. St. John B. Philby, an old friend of Ibn Sa'ud for more than 30 years, was expelled from the country about mid-year. Philby's crime was that he had for some time criticized the new life-styles of the royal family, which was beginning to see the level of oil royalties increasing at an exponential rate. The late king had often been generous with money that he often did not have; the new king was even more generous with the vast new amounts that began to pour into the coffers of his treasury. Meanwhile, Philby, the man who crossed the Rub Al Khali in 1932, went off to live in Lebanon, still writing of the excesses of the royal family. My father had met him several times in Riyadh and Dhahran, photographed him and was impressed with this true adventurer. British, a Moslem, brilliant but quite quirky, he was the father of Kim Philby, a Soviet spy, the mole who had betrayed his country ever since his recruitment by Moscow while he was a student at Cambridge in the 1930s.

In 1956, King Sa'ud felt confident that he could leave his kingdom without fear of any threats to it and traveled to the United States, visiting President Dwight D. Eisenhower at the White House and making a speech—his first ever—before the United Nations in New York. He got a poor reception in New York City but Washington rolled out the red carpet. My father, then a reporter with the Staten Island Advance, wrote a three-part feature on the king, his country, and the oil industry during this visit, using a number of his photographs. He also provided the New York Times with a brief news article and several pictures. The pictures were soon used in an impressive two-page spread in the Times Sunday Magazine, but its editorial department preferred to rely on its Middle East correspondent for the text. With the $250 earned for the pix/story, my father splurged much of it on a high-fidelity record player in an impressive, floor model case. Stereo was still a few years away.

Sometime in 1958, we had a surprise visit from Michael Cheney, a writer with Aramco's public relations department, who my father had worked with on several assignments in the field. Apparently

Downtown, Al Khobar.

he had resigned from the company a year or so before. My parents were delighted to see him and eager to learn what he had been doing since leaving Arabia. Well, he had written a book, and presented us with one of the first copies. It was a 282-page, hard-cover book, called Big Oil Man From Arabia, and published by Ballentine Books, New York. It contained about a dozen photographs, several of them taken by my father, others by Tommy Walters. None carried any credits, as Mike felt that Aramco and the Saudi government might object. He had spent the last few days with his publisher in Manhattan, and had been presented with several copies for his use. When he left us, he flew to California to rejoin his wife Margaret (Maggie) and daughter Victoria. She was three years older than me.

As for the book, which I read many years later, it was a quite comprehensive recapitulation of Michael's time and experiences there, written with a nice low-key sense of humor, as the title of the book might indicate. It was full of facts and details that only he could possible know—except for one deliberate omission. Again for reasons of privacy, concern over various incidents and revelations, Michael had chosen not to identify too many people still working in Arabia. Perhaps it was just as well. It was to be the first of several books to be written by former Aramcons—working stiffs and top brass, as my father characterized them. It was received very well, too.

High-rise apartments, Al Khobar.

Months later we learned that Mike had written a full-length piece in the Saturday Evening Post, entitled, "My Daughter Is An Arab." We obtained a copy and read every word of it. Naturally, the story was all about their daughter Vicky, who was born in Arabia and, as Mike intimated, she had an option to secure Saudi Arabian citizenship if she so desired at some later point in her life. It was illustrated with pictures taken by Mike or Maggie and was sort of a fun piece, my parents thought. I was impressed because my situation was exactly the same as Vickie's except that she was a few years older than me, about eleven years to my seven at that time. I'm not sure if she ever opted in; I know I never did!

In 1964—the world learned that King Sa'ud had been persuaded to yield the throne to his younger half-brother, Faisal. While this may have been interpreted as foreshadowing the coming of one or more

cataclysmic events in the Saudi nation, this transfer of power took place in a relatively calm environment. No doubt Aramco's top management (ensconced in Dhahran since 1952) heaved a collective sign of relief, as did much of the oil-consuming world. It was almost uncanny that life went on in Dhahran, Ras Tanura, Abqaiq, pretty much as usual. With the rest of the world convinced that the government of Saudi Arabia was precariously poised for calamities of some sort or another, King Faisal introduced numerous managerial measures and imposed financial disciplines that proved beneficial in important ways.

In that same year, there was an awful air tragedy that took the lives of 42 Aramcons, many known to my father. One in particular—Bill Scott, manager of Aramco's public relations department—had worked with my father on a story of several of the first Saudis who attended the American University of Beirut (AUB), where Bill taught journalism. Bill then joined Aramco and eventually headed up the department, later introducing television to Saudi Arabia. He had asked my father about job prospects there, and my father urged him to talk to Homer Metz or Jack Butler. Within a couple of months, Bill was in Dhahran.

As for Mike and with the publication of his story in the Post, a prestigious magazine, it looked as though he was on the path to becoming a successful, well-regarded writer and we looked forward to seeing more of his stuff down the road. Sadly, it was not to be: later on, some time in 1960, I believe, we learned that he had died. We understood that, overwhelmed upon discovering he had cancer, Mike had committed suicide. My parents were shocked.

For us, life was undergoing changes. We moved to Minneapolis in 1973, my father once again involved in the oil business, which subsequently led to a ten-year affiliation with a company that took him right back to Arabia—if only for a few weeks. It offered him a chance to fulfil a goal denied him a quarter of a century earlier. In 1989, it seemed within his grasp.

My father had traveled to some of the larger cities and the small towns and villages in Arabia, had been exposed to certain levels of the Saudi government and the royal family, spent time in the desert with exploration crews and observed—if not actually experienced—the harsh, precarious life of the nomadic Bedouin, so one might think he'd seen all he could see. Enough, one might think, to satisfy anyone.

Not so.

His greatest disappointment was that he never got to visit the Rub Al Khali, in English known as the Empty Quarter. The Bedouin called it, simply, the Sands. The Empty Quarter was immense, a vast sea of huge, constantly shifting red sand dunes, thousands of square miles of nothingness. No man or beast lived there permanently, vegetation to sustain life was virtually nonexistent, not a single life-giving stream coursed through this wilderness, the annual rainfall negligible. It offered such intrepid adventurers—the likes of Bertram Thomas and H. St. John B. Philby— nothing but trackless wastes, a blinding, blistering sun by day and frigid temperatures at night with only the stars for company and to offer hope, apparently just the sort of stuff they lived for. It appeared to have no purpose or value to man, whether he be Bedouin, explorer, geologist, or oil driller (at least not then). So my father was not alone in being denied a chance to see it, visit it, fear it—and survive it.

But in 1979, my father, by now a public relations consultant, learned that one of his clients had been invited by Aramco to build a road into the Empty Quarter. S.J. Groves & Sons, based in Minneapolis, was one of the largest privately owned highway and heavy constructions companies in the world. It built everything: highways, dams, tunnels, bridges, and hydroelectric plants. It mined coal, gold, silver, oil shale in America and abroad. In all of these extractive processes, the company learned over 75 years how to move dirt quickly, expeditiously, economically—and profitably. It was usually the first thing that happened whenever another major element of this nation's basic infrastructure was conceived, designed, and bid out to construction firms. It had an unparalleled reputation for performance and integrity. It partnered itself with Guy F. Atkinson, a U.S. firm, and Tamimi & Fouad, a very reputable Saudi firm based in Al Khobar.

Groves was going to excavate, move, perhaps even shape, millions of cubic feet of sand that had never felt the blade of a bulldozer pushing and moving it out of the way, in the process of cutting a highway into the Empty Quarter.

It looked as though my father, who was asked to go out to write stories and take pictures of this operation, might yet penetrate this colossal sea of sand. He made plans to go to once the equipment

Emergency highway radio phones.

had reached the field and was heading for the giant dunes.

But for some reason, Aramco put the project on hold. Groves was, nevertheless, invited to carry out other projects that required the skills of a heavy construction company. Such as building GOSP (gas and oil separating plant) platforms, fencing in a new airport and others facilities; building a new golf course, and laying some new roads. This was a far cry from Groves's original— and monumental—assignment but the company went to work. Indeed, not long after, on its own initiative and investment, it purchased a complete asphalt manufacturing plant and shipped it out to Al Khobar. Soon operational, it quickly began running at near-maximum production.

The past caught up with my parents in a sad way. On February 10, 1979, while listening to the evening news on television, they read a line of copy superimposed over the TV picture: "Los Angeles Times journalist Joe Alex Morris killed in Teheran." This was the first my parents had heard of Joe in some time. It brought to mind the early days in 1953, when Mossadegh was overthrown, when Joe was a writer in Aramco's public relations department. This time it was the era of the Ayatollah Khomeini, the taking of the American Embassy, whose staff was held hostage for 444 days. Joe, 51, was killed observing a confrontation between Iranian air force cadets and regular soldiers, apparently by a stray bullet.

The Empty Quarter project was further delayed. My father did go out and spent three weeks in the field, photographing various projects, interviewing employees and their families. He saw the new city of Jubail pegged out on the desert, and was overwhelmed at what had taken place in the last quarter of a century. He met Saudis and Americans he had known a quarter of a century ago, most of them still hale and hearty. He flew to Jiddah to have dinner with his old boss, W. Jack Butler, and his wife Pat. Back home, he devoted a special edition of the company's magazine to its men and women working in Arabia. But the Rub Al Khali had been denied him, yet again.

Another 20 years later, in the year 2000, the Saudi Arabian government opened the kingdom to those former employees of Aramco, their wives, and children, who would like to visit the country where

they had lived, worked, and attended school. More than 2,000 past residents signed up, including my mother and me. My father was unable to get away for the two-week trip. We flew into Bahrain late at night, climbed into busses and took the 15-kilometer causeway into Al Khobar where we checked into the Hotel AlGosaibi (five-stars), right next door to the even more fabulous Hotel Meridian. "Things have certainly changed," my mother exclaimed.

Not everything. The heat was enveloping, almost overwhelming. We went to a mall that served women (and children) exclusively (not a man in the place). The sales people did not wear the abaya, revealing handsome, beautiful women at the counters. There were bus trips to Ras Tanura and Half Moon Bay. We went into Dhahran and attended presentations by Aramco. We walked about Al Khobar and saw the remains of the Khobar Towers. One day we were invited to a dinner, set in the desert, in air-conditioned tents. Large, bright multihued rugs were strewn on the desert floor. Great circular metal platters of rice were placed about us. Imbedded in them were whole sheep or goats. We sat cross-legged, and ate in the traditional style of the Bedouin (sans cutlery). The interior was quiet, full of light, and blessedly cool.

But we were running out of time. Advised that we could visit either Jiddah, on the Red Sea, or go south to Shaybah, a drilling site deep in the Rub Al Khali, there was no discussion. The Empty Quarter was for us. Early the following morning we boarded a shiny silver plane and within an hour or so, the flat, tannish desert gave way to deep reddish sand that began to grow higher and higher, taking the form of ever larger sand dunes, the morning light casting long, dense black shadows about them.

Birth of vast new industrial complex.

Then we came upon a huge depression in the desert with a collection of structures, each one a different shape or size, dotted about its floor, surrounded by high red dunes that looked as though they would swallow up everything in sight, if they desired. Our plane made a perfect landing, came to a halt and we stepped out of its cool interior. An incredible wave of heat hit us. It was 113 degrees in the shade.

I could now go home and tell my father that even though he had

Adventurers, All!

H. St. John B. Philby.

Historians are unclear as to who should be credited with being the first adventurer to penetrate the heartland of Arabia. Rome at some point did mount an expedition in search of one more nation or landmass to colonize and exploit, this time failing for the lack of water, it seems.

Of merchants down through the ages there were many who established routes that intersected with or were close to the larger cities, towns, and villages; or even established markets to sell or barter the exotica of the day: herbs, spices, salt, cloth and other essentials. None could be called "adventurers", their goal was commerce. In due course the Bedouin in the hinterlands came to town for his few needs. He paid for them with livestock, milk, or other by-products from his camels, goats, or sheep, returning to his cruel, precarious lifestyle, contemptuous of the merchant's soft life, beholden only to his family, his tribe, his gods, and a little banditry now and then. He was a free man, in charge of his own destiny, bleak though it surely was.

Thus the desert slumbered on for centuries more, baking and boiling beneath an unrelenting sun, the land yielding little to sustain these tribes. In the seventh century came Mohammed and Islam, which for the next several hundred years carried out its own unique form of adventuring, though its monumental impact on the Western world did little to improve the material lot of the nomad.

With the advent of national adventurism, better known as imperialism in the eighteenth century, there emerged

At Udhailiyah, this bevy of camels insisted on being photographed. Unhobbled with their owners nowhere in sight, they regularly arranged themselves in interesting tableaux, finally assembling on a slight sandy rise in a pose that could not be ignored.

a breed of individual who set out to make his (or her) mark on those remaining places in the world, so far un-

explored. Educated, often idiosyncratic, and occasionally wealthy enough to underwrite the expense of such explorations, a good number of them were English.

Consequently, Arabia Felix has suffered over time its full measure of such explorers: anthropologists, scientists, authors, journalists, photographers, missionaries, businessmen, politicians, and a few charlatans, to boot. Indeed, I believe I have met a few of them. They came to observe, exploit if possible, and, eventually, to marvel. For such were the extremes of nature they came upon—that incessant sun, the virtually cloudless sky, the immeasurable shimmering desertscapes, a land that could not boast a single, perennial stream or river—most were awed if not overwhelmed.

So they returned home to establish or further burnish reputations, lecture before scientific institutions, or write articles or books to satisfy newspaper's or publisher's needs. From which flowed money, medals, fame, and honors bestowed by a grateful nation. Few, if any set up permanent residence there.

Such people as Sir Richard Burton come to mind. His almost clinical fascination with pornography led to expeditions to the Near, Middle, and Far East during the 1890s. Along the way, he translated the Kama Sutra, the erotic literature of India, the classic Arabian fairy tale, Aladdin and His Wonderful Lamp, and A Thousand and One Nights. Among his many audacious exploits, unquestionably his most outrageous was that of representing himself—an infidel—as a Moslem and penetrating the holy

---

(left) Most adventurers sought the past (antiquity, archeology, architecture) but the mythic riches eluded them. Aramco honored the past and found Saudi Arabia's wealth beneath its sandy wastes.

cities of Mecca and Medina, to witness the Haj. It was dangerous but something he obviously enjoyed doing.

He escaped with his life; his book, <u>Pilgrimage to Mecca and Medina</u>, was published in 1893, after his death in 1890. It was edited by his wife, Lady Isabel Burton (who destroyed all of the erotica immediately following his demise).

Another grand personality was Richard D. Doughty, author of <u>Travels in Arabia Deserta</u>. A massive tome published in 1888, it remains the definitive travel book about Arabia to this day. He suffered harshly, precariously, in researching it, living on and off for years with Bedouin tribes, principally in the Nedj. Welcomed by some, beaten unmercifully by others, and once abandoned in the desert by a treacherous guide (a virtual death sentence) he, nevertheless, prevailed. Even the Turks arrested him, stole his materials and belongings, but eventually released him and returned his precious documents. A canny individual, it appears that he frequently identified himself as a doctor, carrying pills and other medications of the day, as well as nostrums of his own concoction. His judicious dispensing of them may have saved his life on more than one occasion.

Gertrude Bell, on the other hand, was a rare, rich aristocratic beauty with an Oxford degree who spoke Arabic fluently. She became a powerful and influential member of the Colonial Office headed by Winston Churchill. He and Ms. Bell are credited with creating Iraq in just one afternoon, cutting up the former Ottoman Empire into various pieces (using an old map, scissors and a pot of paste) to satisfy the principal victors of the Great War. She even fashioned a flag for the newly-minted country and helped select its new king.

Ms. Bell, as Oriental secretary, traveled widely, and reputedly was the first Western woman to meet the future king of Saudi Arabia

The Americans cast a long, enduring shadow for 75 years.

(then emir of the Nedj), and she was the first one he had met to make a very good impression on him, by all the evidence available. She was apparently invaluable, knowing more of the regions' many tribes and their leaders than any man. It was adventure of a high order, where she was perfectly comfortable and almost an equal among the power brokers of that period. A museum in her name might still exist in Baghdad.

On the other hand, Freya Stark, a fragile Englishwoman from the county of Dorset, knew as a child that she wished to escape into an emptier, less fretful life than the hurly-burly of cosmopolitan, industrial England. Later on, she more sharply defined her goal as that "place where space, distance, history, and danger exists." Somewhat prescient, she felt that oil was going to play an important part in her life, which was closer to the truth than she had imagined.

In poor health much of her life, she hugged the western coastline of Arabia, rarely venturing into the central portions, sickness often accompanying her as she explored the Hadhramaut, a special interest. Slim lyrical volumes, extraordinarily detailed and beautifully illustrated, such as the <u>Valley of Assassins</u>, and <u>A Winter In Arabia</u>, testify to this tiny woman's aggressive devotion to her subject.

Another Oxford student, T.E. Lawrence, walked Syria over a two-

year period and served as a subaltern in the British army upon the coming of the Great War. His knowledge of that region served him well, enabling him to organize several Bedouin tribes in raids against Turkish forces. His successes, though modest, were extravagantly publicized by Lowell Thomas, an American newspaperman from Butte, Montana, who put both himself and "Lawrenz of Arabia" on the map for all time. <u>The Seven Pillars of Wisdom</u>, written by Lawrence and published in 1926 revealed a tortured individual whose genuine efforts to serve the cause of the Arabs came to nought because of the cynicism of the French and British.

An American, Carleton S. Coon, a Minnesotan and author, visited Arabia several times, conducting research on a number of tribes, but for some reason was asked to leave (perhaps his wartime service in the OSS and subsequent affiliations may have had a bearing on his eventual expulsion).

None of these people, save one, spent much of his entire life in Arabia. The exception was H. St. John B. Philby, who was born in Norfolk, grew up in Essex, and was a true adventurer who did it all: He was a soldier, diplomat, Arabist, explorer, businessman, author, and a Moslem. Some even say he was a spy; his son Kim certainly was. The greatest role he played was that of counselor to King Ibn Sa'ud, who for many years required Philby's presence at his daily court in Riyadh, and who sought his advice until his death in 1953 about the political subtleties and imperial practices of the British government, with which Philby still had close ties, despite many differences with it. Philby crossed the Rub Al Khali in 1932, accompanied by soldiers and guides provided by Ibn Sa'ud, achieving a goal that had eluded him for many years.

But he was not the first to do so, to Philby's anger and utter disgust that honor fell to Bertram Sidney Thomas, who had crossed the previous year (February 1931) without benefit of the protection of Ibn Sa'ud's soldiers. Indeed, he did not even seek permission from Ibn Sa'ud, moving quickly and in a straight line from Salal on the South coast to Doha on the Arabian Gulf. It was thought that Thomas had once been a subordinate of Philby's, which really must have galled him.

Thomas was of the same general mold as Philby. Born in 1892 near Bristol, he was a fellow commoner at Trinity College, Cambridge, then went off to serve in the Great War, both on the Western Front and the Near East. A sojourn in Mesopotamia caught his soul, which eventually led to him to becoming the finance minister (and wazir) to the sultan of Muscat and Oman. During this interlude, he made several excursions into the desert, which prepared him for the eventual penetration of the Empty Quarter. His book, Arabia Felix, covered this extraordinary exploit. He won medals and honors from his government, and died in Cairo on December 27, 1950, a relatively young man of 58.

Another chap, Wilfrid Thesiger, who the New York Times noted "was among the last of the great explorers lucky enough to have lived when the globe still had some uncharted corners," died just two years ago in Surrey, England, at age 93. He was the only man to have traversed the Rub Al Khali twice, first in 1946 and then again in 1948. He too had all the right things at his fingertips: wealth, Eton and Oxford, influence in that part of the world. An accomplished photographer, he illustrated his several books with striking black and white photographs. He was what we would today call a loner, one who readily discarded the substance and security of the modern world and found contentment in the desert of the Bedouin. He hated the arrival of oil rigs, pipelines, and four-wheeled drive automobiles, all of which destroyed forever the life that he admired.

But when the Americans came along and sought a concession to drill for oil, Philby was the man to see. He was, surprisingly, in their corner from the very start, spiting his own government in the arduous process. His role as their friend at Ibn Sa'ud's court paved the way for such an agreement, although it took a couple of years to secure. Oddly enough, he did not become immensely wealthy as might be his due. He was quirky, utterly candid, wrote it all down—then put it into print, costing him dearly along the way.

As for the Americans, they brought, bought, or built everything they needed for a long stay. And stay they did, under one flag (CASOC), then another (Aramco), for nearly 75 years. And they will, no doubt, be serving the Saudi government under its new name (Saudi Aramco), for many more years to come.

Only the Americans stayed.

It was a colossal gamble at that time, when oil was selling on the open market at 75 cents a barrel—a barrel, not a gallon. (A barrel is 62 gallons.) Who in Heaven's name needed more oil? Only other oil people, it seemed.

It is almost impossible to plot out the thought processes of the

board members that made such a decision, no doubt overcoming the fears or reluctance of a few who saw, perhaps, nothing but more dry holes for the company. They had also to face the prospect of entering Saudi Arabia, in which they had no experience whatsoever, was seven thousands miles away, and whose bleak, inhospitable and barren lands (rather, deserts) would demand the introduction of Americans in large numbers, if the oil company had any real hopes of keeping people there for months, even years at a time, to get back its investment and keep stockholders satisfied.

Perhaps the economics of it all might make sense in time, if first the nation could get out of the greatest economic crisis it had ever experienced. The profits that would flow if oil were to be found in commercial quantities was a tantalizing thought to conjure with.

The company, Socal, counted on ten men—several geologists, then men with a combination of essential skills such as a mechanic/photographer/boatman and other special talents—to form the advance guard. They went out to confirm some encouraging signs, suspicions, or even convictions of Fred A. Davies. Another geologist, Max Steineke, not one of the original ten, asked his bosses at Socal to send him to Arabia. It wasn't long before everyone recognized that Max "was the man who came to understand the stratigraphy and the structure underlying eastern Arabia's nearly featureless surface," as noted by Wallace Stegner in his book Discovery!

Socal continued to commit the enormous monies that would fund a foolhardy undertaking that would within a generation be characterized as fulfilling every expectation of the company and earning the respect of the oil industry and the world. Steineke never saw much of this, dying in 1948.

So the Americans came and stayed and stayed and stayed. For nearly three generations, making an impact on the Kingdom of Saudi Arabia that has never been matched in any other part of the world.

On a pretty street in Dhahran, surrounded by mature trees and flowering bushes, sits a handsome brick structure that is used by visitors from all over the world when they visit Aramco. It is called the Max Steineke Guest House.

'Dry Holes' in Dammam

The company—CASOC—was in search of cash. In the middle months of 1941, a young, under challenged cartographer started looking about for a more interesting, perhaps even defense-related, assignment that might put his talents to better use. A war was going on in Europe, begun when Great Britain, honoring its treaty obligation to Poland (invaded on September 1, 1939), had, two days later, declared war on Nazi Germany. Isolationist America watched, but Pearl Harbor was not far off.

Ray T. Graham, 24, had finally joined the U.S. Geological Survey Department, following a disappointing search for something that might put all his talents to good use. He found himself shuffling hundreds of aerial photographs that had been taken of several western states, the first photographic documentary of that region. He worked the 4 to 12 shift, which gave him most of the day to look for another position. With a Master of Fine Arts degree from Yale, he needed to move on.

Someone suggested he apply at the War Manpower Commission. Graham appeared before a committee of men who were apparently going to be interviewing a large number of candidates that day. The first and almost obligatory question directed at him was:

"Son, where are you from?'"

"Sir, I'm from Oklahoma."

"Well, so am I," said his questioner.

"Do you know anything about the oil industry," was the next question, posed by the same person.

"I grew up in it, sir," was the answer.

With that, this man reached into his waistcoat pocket, extracted a business card, wrote something on the back of it and slid the piece of white pasteboard across the table to Graham. "Go see this gentleman," he said.

Graham did as he was told, met the man, who sent him on to another man, whose name was J. Terry Duce. Duce was an internationally known geologist and the executive vice president of the Texas Oil Company, which had loaned him to the U. S. government to begin to organize the oil industry through the creation of the Petroleum Administration for War, headed up by Harold L. Ickes, secretary of the interior, just named by Franklin D. Roosevelt as petroleum coordinator for national defense. Duce and Ralph K. Davies had invited 74 heads of small and large oil companies from around the nation to come to Washington to be briefed on what the government needed to do, with their cooperation. That meeting was about two weeks away and Duce needed help. His staff were already busily producing a great deal of data that would be used at the gathering, but Duce knew that it had to presented in ways that could be quickly understood, digested, and retained

CASOC

There was no time for a fancy logo.

by such busy executives. He needed to put on a powerful, dramatic presentation, using striking visual aids: charts, graphs, graphics, Illustrations, whatever was necessary to keep these men focussed. Could Mr. Graham help him. Ray said he was sure he could.

*****

Ray Graham had indeed grown up in the oil industry, in California and Oklahoma. He was born in 1916 as a twin (his brother's name was Roy) to Hattie (nee Isom) and Wray in Coalinga, 160 miles southeast of San Francisco. Their sister, Margaret, was born two years earlier. Wray Graham was a successful oil wildcatter and with his brothers developed California Oilfields Limited at Coalinga, which was subsequently sold for $13 million to Shell Oil Company. Ray's father moved the family to Pershing, nine miles south of Pawhuska, Oklahoma, and the capital of the Osage Nation in 1918. They lived on a ranch in a 14-room natural stone house, originally built for the chief justice of the supreme court of the Cherokee Nation, where he brought in 74 producing oil wells. Pershing was proud of its new citizens and agreed to rename the town Graham if the company paved the main street.

The Grahams borrowed $1 million from the Standard Oil Company of New Jersey and built a refinery. The Great War ended at the eleventh hour of the eleventh day of the eleventh month in 1918. Wray Graham spent three years in Texas wildcatting at the height of exploration. With the continued fall in the price of a barrel of oil and with failing health he went broke and died at the age of 33 leaving a 29-year old widow and three children.

Hattie moved to Fairfax and became a beautician. She then sold that shop and bought a hotel in Ponca City (home of the Ponca Indians), which often had baseball teams (sponsored by oil companies) come in from Nebraska to play local teams. One such firm—the E.W. Marlin Company, eventually absorbed by Conoco—fielded a team, which frequently stayed at her hotel. Mrs. Graham wound up marrying the third baseman. The next stop was at Shawnee where she opened another hotel, which failed. It seems that for each school grade the children lived in a different town, finally moving to Oklahoma City where they completed junior high and senior high school.

Then Ray (and Roy) entered Oklahoma University as fine arts majors. Ray paid for his education by working as the resident designer for the Oklahoma City Scenic Company, which had clients in 24 states. In 1936, he went out to Los Angeles to attend a summer session at the Chouniard School of Art to study motion picture design. He discovered that he could draft and draw but would never be an illustrator. Not one but two professors urged him to go to Yale, which is what he did in 1939. Shortly after America entered the war he came to Washington and, rejected by the Selective Service Boards because of pierced eardrums (both he and Roy had had chronic ear problems throughout their childhood), filed with the Civil Service Commission in search of a job. He became a somewhat reluctant cartographer, making $200 more a year than his brother was making elsewhere.

*****

Ray explained his situation to Duce and suggested that for the next two weeks he moonlight the job. He also pointed out that the assignment was going to require an awful lot of handlettering, in addition to the numerous other tasks associated with the project that he would be overseeing. He said he wanted to employ two girls, fellow employees who were excellent letterers. Former employees of Hallmark Greeting Cards, in Kansas, they would be crucial to the success of the presentation. Hire them, said Duce.

In short order, following the success of that meeting, Ray set up a graphic design unit in the office of John Thatcher, who was executive secretary to Ralph Davies, former president and chairman of the Standard Oil Company of California, then serving as deputy petroleum administrator, under Ickes. By the end of the war, Ray had hired about 20 people to handle the work.

About this time Davies called in Ray and said he wanted him to meet, in New York, a William F. Moore who was heading up a division of Socal, called California Arabian Oil Standard Oil Company (which was by this time fifty percent owned by Texas Oil Company). CASOC was in Saudi Arabia, drilling for oil at several points on the mainland, but with little or no luck.

Ray flew to New York, met with Moore, who told him that CASOC was running out of money and needed to raise $400 million dollars to stay in the game. The former cartographer put together a presentation for use before eleven major banks in New York. That same presentation was shipped to San Francisco, whereupon Mobil Oil Company and Standard Oil of New Jersey were invited to come aboard. The final division of CASOC was 30 percent Texas Oil Company, 30 percent Socal, 30 percent Standard Oil, and 10 percent Mobil. The monies fueled a tremendous expansion program in Arabia. Oil in commercial quantities had been discovered in 1933.

Thus began for Ray and Roy Graham (as Graham Associates) a return to the oil industry, an affiliation that lasted almost 60 years, many of them with the newly-named Arabian American Oil Company and in other years with other oil companies and organizations in the Middle East, as Aramco's retrenchment programs in the sixties came into play.

The range of services provided by Graham Associates was quite extraordinary. Its prewar exposure to the oil industry—and the ability to provide the top levels of that industry with what it needed in a timely fashion—established it as an organization that could do the same thing in a postwar environment. The important point to keep in mind was that working with talented people of all types—photographers, graphic designers, writers, film producers, and every other imaginable creative process—was not what the oil executives wanted to do with their valuable time. What they were looking for, and were not always sure how to find, was someone who knew their industry, could manage these disparate creative resources, and get the job done. What better than the son of a wildcatter with an Ivy League degree, coupled not only with innate creative talents, but also with the discipline to manage the talents of others. He and his brother Roy, equally resourceful, in the form of Graham Associates, was the answer, it seemed to many.

Over time, Graham Associates, based in Washington, D.C., worked with most of the people who were hired by CASOC and subsequently Aramco The early programs carried out by the public relations departments in San Francisco and New York were modest, initially directed at internal audiences, assisted by Ray and Roy Graham. A number of regional events—political, economic, religious—that quickly became world concerns, called for a major expansion of the communications activities of Aramco. The Grahams were ready and willing, assisting management in producing training manuals, employee booklets, newsletters, and much more printed materials.

The early fifties was the greatest period of communications activity in Aramco. While its New York public relations department remained essentially the same size, the office in the field grew appreciably, adding writers and photographers (still and motion picture), to service the growing requests for pictures and stories about all aspects of the oil operations and the Americans living and working in Saudi Arabia.

It wasn't long before Graham Associates decided to set up shop in Beirut, Lebanon, this occurring in 1952. It reasoned that a first-class printing operation could prosper, serving any number and variety of clients (one of which was Aramco). Serendipitously, at the continued urging of the Saudi government, the headquarters of Aramco was moved from Manhattan to Dhahran, requiring a number of key executives to establish homes in Arabia. An exception to this was the PR department, which needed to maintain strong and immediate contacts with all forms of print media, most of these based in Manhattan, center of that universe.

Print was paramount in serving most of the world, whether by teletype, newsprint, magazines, simple black and white folders, or elaborate four-color brochures. But not in Saudi Arabia, where literacy was low and the learning curve for Arabic and English was exceedingly extended. Film, narrated in Arabic, was the obvious answer to this near-crippling communication challenge, which H.O. Thompson and W. J. Butler, Aramco's PR management in New York and Dhahran were eager to exploit, expanding on the earlier successes begun in 1948 in producing educational films on water and malaria for Aramco's medical department.

Over the next 15 years, Graham Associates produced about 40 films of all types for various departments in Aramco, including several more for Dr. Richard Daggy, a specialist in malarial diseases who eventually became head of Aramco's medical services. Then someone came up with the idea of producing a feature film, one suitable for possible distribution to world audiences. It was called Jazirat al-Arab, Island of the Arabs, its central focus being the consolidation of Arabia under Ibn Sa'ud. It was directed by Richard Lyford, a former director with Walt Disney Studios, using all sorts of Aramco employees in various roles. The king was played by John Rufus Jones, a big fellow as large and as powerful-looking as Saud. A member of the government relations department, he carried it off wonderfully well but got no calls from Hollywood. Plus he spoke Arabic, a multitalented guy. Isa Sabbagh, a WW II BBC announcer, gave it all a credibility that was valuable.

The movie had gala premiers in Cairo and Alexandria with searchlights, personalities (even a couple of real movie stars), and numerous guests of Aramco. In the Middle East, it got some good distribution and press coverage. Gamel Abdel Nasser was president of Egypt at the time.

As for the rest of the world, it didn't break too many box-office records in such places as New York City or Hollywood, but it was well done and deserved credit for its production values and accuracy. See page 110 for "Making Movies in Hollywood or Hofuf." Film was now a powerful element in the ever-more sophisticated communication processes of Aramco. Television was still a few years away, though.

The Middle East's reception of the film was encouraging to Aramco and Riyadh, which came to understand the value of communicating on a regular basis with its neighbors. Meanwhile, an exhibit prepared for an international fair that was held in Damascus, which featured the roles of Aramco and particularly Tapline (which ran through several countries) went over well. Several Saudi's served as guides and explained the exhibits to visitors from all around the world, a new and important role that put these young men up front for the rest of the world to see. The exhibit returned year after year, revised and expanded, for ten years. It was a success and went onto other points—Beirut and Bahrain, for example.

Meanwhile, with such success came encouragement to do more, presumably with bigger budgets to support other proposals of the public relations department.

Butler, manager of the department, recognizing that the success of the external exhibitions could succeed just as well within the borders of Arabia—if the government could be persuaded—recommended that a similar effort be designed for the interior, and won approval for a similar exhibit or show. However, this one would be mobile, so designed that it could travel throughout the kingdom, bringing it to key towns and cities such as Jiddah, Riyadh, Asir, Quatif, and Hofuf, as well as smaller towns and villages. A travelling road show, in effect.

Better still, it became a portable tent show, uniquely designed by Ray Graham to enclose a marvelous array of exhibits. They documented not only the process of the oil business but also the accomplishments of Americans and Saudis working together in the nation's oil industry. Also, but for the first time the exhibit reminded the Saudis and visitors of the cultural heritage of the entire Middle East. And film played an important role, as short features on many subjects were screened daily. The public was impressed, young Saudis felt considerable pride at the accomplishments of their countrymen, some even wondering if they could find employment in it. The tent show went on for several years.

But other, important development were taking place in Riyadh, Dhahran, New York, and indeed around the world, all connected to oil. During the latter part of the decade (1958), King Sa'ud yielded authority for many of the executive functions of government to his brother, Prince Faysal, although the king remained until 1964. W. Jack Butler, who had spent nearly ten years in Arabia and felt that he had put in place one of the most comprehensive public relations program ever in a foreign company, resigned in 1959.

Shortly thereafter, Harold O. "Tommy" Thompson, vice president of Aramco's public relations office in New York, resigned. (See "Keeper of the Gates", page 26.) Finally, an oil glut that had been threatening world markets showed up, bringing about retrenchment programs in many areas at Aramco, including public relations.

It was about that same time for Graham Associates to sever its connections with Aramco and Saudi Arabia, concluding an affiliation of more than a quarter of a century. It went on to even greater involvement with the Middle East, including impressive assignments with Esso Libya. They produced several new films and a brilliant exhibit entitled Heritage of Islam which opened at the Smithsonian Institution, Washington, D.C., and traveled to other major cities in America in 1981. For almost another 25 years, Ray Graham remained a resource for American oil companies engaged in or connected with the oil industry in the Middle East.

Now, retired for several years, and living in New York and Florida, he is not forgotten. In 2002, he was invited to a dinner in Washington, D.C. by Abdallah Jum'ah, president and chief executive officer of Saudi Aramco. (See "Aramco Is No More," page 114.)

Keeper of the Gates

Ibn Sa'ud Gave Aramco the Keys to the Kingdom.

For Ibn Sa'ud, the road to the consolidation of much of the Arabian Peninsula into a unified kingdom that rightfully took his name was long, arduous, and bloody—but of only passing interest to the outside world. It began in 1902, when he and a band of Bedouin fighters stormed down from Kuwait to seize Riyadh in the middle of the night.

The path that King Ibn Sa'ud took to eventually secure fabulous oil riches for his nation was much shorter, though equally arduous in the seemingly never-ending negotiations of the minute details of the oil concession agreement. No blood was shed as far as can be ascertained, but it did generate a lot of heat and perspiration in the process. Actually, Ibn Sa'ud was skeptical about the benefits of finding oil and was more concerned about drilling for water, which he felt his new nation needed even more desperately than oil.

In 1923, his first agreement with Major Frank Holmes, a New Zealander, came to nought, as the British syndicate in London that he represented failed to convince any oil company that there might be oil in Arabia. The concession agreement lapsed as interest waned and the money dried up. The world yawned.

Seven years later—in 1930—Charles R. Crane, an American who had become extremely wealthy through his business of selling bathtubs, bidets, sinks, and toilets

to the world, and had a philanthropic 'soft spot' for the Middle East, offered to send the king a qualified engineer (Karl S. Twitchell, a doughty New Englander) to explore

Shaikh Abdullah Bulkhair and W. Jack Butler meet in Cairo, Egypt.

and quantify, if possible, the water, minerals, and oil resources of Arabia. Twitchell's two-year search of portions of the mainland brought disappointing news for both Crane and the king, although he had become fascinated—and ultimately extremely wealthy—as he focussed his energies on the search for gold.

The times were tough.

It was 1932 and the Great Depression was in its fourth year, the economies of the world in shambles, with catastrophic dislocation of the leading nations' financial markets, and vast unemployment across every segment of society. Even Saudi Arabia felt the pinch. A prime source of Saud's income was the annual Haj, the yearly pilgrimage by Moslems from all over the world, who came to worship at the holy cities of Mecca and Medina. Over a period of several years, the number of pilgrims had dropped by 40 percent, posing a grim hardship for a government constantly in need of funds.

In May of that same year, Standard Oil of California finally struck oil in commercial quantities on the tiny island of Bahrain, in the Persian Gulf, some 15 miles due east of the Arabian coastline. The oil company, through a series of byzantine connections, obscure developments, and defaults by other American oil companies, had become the first major U.S. oil company to secure in 1928 an exclusive agreement to explore there for oil. Fred A. Davies, from St. Paul, Minnesota, the lead geologist on Bahrain, urged his management to seek permission from the Saudi government to explore the mainland, specifically the portion of the coastline that could be seen from his vantage point on Bahrain. They agreed, probably reluctantly, as the average cost of a barrel of oil at that time in the United States was 75 cents. It was a great gamble but they put their faith in Davies' hunch that the geological formations present on the island might extend to the Arabian mainland. It smacked of wildcatting in Texas or Oklahoma. An initial approach to the Saudi government was made and rejected. Another one, with the ubiquitous

H. St. John B. Philby involved, secured an invitation to visit Arabia and meet with King Ibn Sa'ud and various of his counselors. Philby, an adventurer of the type Britain produced in quantity, assured the king that Americans would be easier to work with than the English. He turned up at several of the meetings with the government and was helpful to the Americans in many ways, deliberately slighting some rather halfhearted efforts by the British, who wanted to stay in the game but not make any major investment.

Howard Beir, publicist.

Apparently the king agreed. Indeed, he had been quoted as saying that he actually liked—or at least could tolerate—the Americans because they were so far away. Besides, he'd had enough of the British, who loaned him money, sold him weapons, and consequently felt they had a right to meddle in the politics of the area. He became convinced that U.S. oil companies would focus on finding petroleum, and nothing else, lest the concession agreement be placed in jeopardy. An American negotiating team was dispatched to Jiddah early in 1933. Nearly four months later, after intense negotiations, a concession agreement was signed on May 29 by the finance minister, Shaikh Abdullah Allah Suleiman. The several financial incentives to be provided by the company as part of the agreement—advances, loans and rentals—were to paid in gold. The concession was to run 60 years. Only ten years had passed since Sa'ud had taken the first tentative steps to find oil—or water—in his kingdom.

The great adventure was about to get underway.

The first exploration crew, including Bert Miller and Krug Henry, came ashore in a motor launch at Jubail on September 23, 1933. Dressed in traditional Arab headgear to minimize local attention, they were accompanied by a detachment of soldiers. Other members drove overland from Cairo and Beirut. Nearly two years later, the first well—Dammam #1—drilled on April 30, 1935, was a disappointment, producing only a hundred barrels a day. Dammam #2 was a dry hole. Holes #3, 4, 5 and 6 were not much better. Dammam #7, a deep test hole, was spudded in on December 7, 1937, and proved to be the most cantankerous of them all. Fifteen

months later, on March 22, 1938, the well produced 3,810 barrels a day. Earlier wells were then drilled deeper and proved out. The Dammam field was declared a commercial reality. Ibn Sa'ud was informed and presented with the agreed-upon bonus of $50,000 delivered in gold bullion. Royalties of $1 a ton of oil produced began to flow into the coffers of the finance minister at Jiddah. Initially a dribble, that dribble soon became a steady stream.

The world of business acknowledged these events, noting that Saudi Arabia had joined the ranks of several other Middle East oil producing nations, despite many people wondering just where Arabia was located. The company at that time was known as the California Arabian Standard Oil Company (CASOC), although a name change was in the offing. Even more important was the fact that an American oil company was now firmly in place in a part of the world that was usually thought of as the hunting grounds of the British Empire. Some competitors even labeled it as outright poaching and were sure that it was only a matter of time before the "Americans would come a cropper."

The Depression was still running its course, but the isms of the era—fascism, totalitarianism, and communism—created the perfect conditions for war, a conflagration that took six years to resolve, with the Allies the ultimate winners. During the early days of World War II, CASOC fulfilled its obligations under the concession agreement, continuing to build the infrastructure of a modern oil industry: storage tanks, pipelines, a marine terminal, and a small refinery.

Soon the shortage of raw materials, an abortive bombing raid by the Italian air force on Dhahran in 1940 (the real target was the refinery on Bahrain Island), and the threat of Rommel's continuing advance into Egypt, forced the company to evacuate most of its workers and shut down the bulk of its operations. A hundred or so men remained to provide crude oil to the Bapco Refinery, and to carry out limited maintenance and security for the facilities in Dhahran, Ras Tanura, and Abqaiq. Slowly the Allies gained the upper hand and, as if expressing a vote of confidence in them, on January 31, 1944, the name CASOC was replaced by one that more closely reflected the true nature and quality of this new partnership: the Arabian American Oil Company.

Homer Metz, PR manager, Tapline.

The end of the war in 1945 brought a gradual resumption of activities followed by an extraordinary period of growth for the fledgling oil company, where the potentially immense oil revenues and royalties generated might, according to a few optimists, enable Saudi Arabia to plan and build the fundamental infrastructure essential for a modern industrial nation. This vision (or mirage) could well involve Aramco far beyond its purely petroleum obligations, at least for a generation or so. The growth in royalties, still minuscule in comparison to today's colossal numbers, slowly brought about changes in Riyadh, most beneficial, some not.

****

In the early post-World War II years, nobody questioned the ability of the newly-minted, newly-named Arabian American Oil Company (Aramco) to explore, produce, refine, and transport the petroleum products and derivatives that burst from the desert oil fields. The enormous and diverse resources of its owners (Socal, Exxon, Texaco, and Mobil) underwriting this first truly all-American venture were a guarantee of success, at least from a technological point of view. That was the easy part, relatively speaking, a no-brainer in the colloquial language of today. The drilling of new producing wells in new fields confirmed the owners' wildest dreams: Saudi Arabia was going to prove to be the greatest oil producing country in the history of the oil industry.

After discovery, the next major challenge was finding the manpower to conceive, design, and build a new, state-of-the art petroleum industry in Arabia. The owners could—and did—make available a number of their own people, a cadre of highly qualified oil men in virtually any industry specialty: engineers (civil, mechanical, electrical), geologists, draftsmen, cartographers, administrators, accountants and many more. Beyond absorbing these and others, Aramco set about tapping the pool of talent that existed in the millions of Americans who had returned home on being discharged from the U.S. armed forces.

Finding them was going to be an enormous task but one that was understood and within the scope of Aramco's recruiters, who quickly set up offices in several major cities and began placing ads in local newspapers. To accelerate the gigantic construction program, established international firms, such as Fluor, Bechtel, Brown & Roote, and others, were invited to bid on hundreds of contracts. All of these were predictable tasks that could be readily planned for, engineered, bid out, and scheduled.

The next requirement that the Saudi government was not terribly enthusiastic about was the need to mobilize thousands of Americans who would become permanent residents charged with running the oil operations. A further need was to open up the country to the rest of the world, principally journalists of all types, who sensed that a lot of good stories might be found in this remote, tenth-century land of sand, which had so far permitted entry to only a handful of Westerners, and then only if they served the government's needs. King Ibn Sa'ud and his religious supporters wanted nothing from the West that might corrupt their faith.

Convincing Ibn Sa'ud of the absolute necessity to invite the outside world to come visit his kingdom to marvel at—perhaps—an eighth wonder of the universe, was daunting. It wasn't just the mystery of the exotic Middle East and the existence of Mecca and Medina; the rumors of its fabled oil had also caught the fancy of writers, journalists, and photographers, all in search of good copy and adventure. They were not alone; foreign governments were eager to establish alliances, politicians organized junkets to learn firsthand about Arabia, and businessmen of every stripe, sensing a fabulous new market with instant petrodollars (rather than dubious, long-drawn out credit arrangements) available to pay for their products, geared up for the challenge. Even a few modern-day adventurers showed up. All clamored at the gates for entry to this new phenomenon, for this time the riches were real, taking the forms of crude oil and natural gas in presumably limitless quantities.

But still the major gates to the Kingdom of Arabia—historically at Jiddah and Yanbo on the Red Sea, and latterly at the tiny ports of Dammam, Al Khobar, and Jubail on the Persian Gulf—remained closed to all such visitors, except for those Americans (and Europeans) deemed vital to exploring, extracting, processing, and shipping the oil to the world markets. The government of Saudi Arabia, expressing the inflexible will of King Ibn Sa'ud, determined that the country would remain unsullied by the excesses of the Western world, thereby strictly limiting those who could enter the kingdom. Indeed, those who were permitted to enter Saudi Arabia required the sponsorship of Aramco. They did not need to have an entry visa—but did need an exit visa, which behooved the visitor to closely observe the customs of the country. A neat Machiavellian touch, some thought. For most, the gates remained shut tight, the Saudi government adamant about restricting entry to their kingdom.

This was not a desirable situation for a new oil company with substantial volumes of crude oil products that had to be sold on long-

term contracts in world markets. It was a question of assuming the stability of the country as a secure source of oil. Aramco hastened to persuade the king and his counselors of the vital necessity to open the doors just a crack to permit entry to people who had a legitimate interest in the oil operations of Aramco, were sympathetic to the aspirations of the Saudi, government and people, and would do them no harm.

It was a knotty problem for the Saudi government. For one thing, even if it could be persuaded to be more flexible, it lacked the human resources and worldly perspective that would be necessary to physically manage, let alone understand, the interests and attitudes of the growing number of people lining up at the gates. They mulled over this quandary at great length as they worked with Aramco field management, including its government relations department, whose erudite managers and staff dealt more closely than anyone else with various levels of the government at Dammam, Riyadh, and Jiddah. Well aware of the sensitivities and potential dangers inherent in handling a flood of visitors but with no experience in this highly specialized field, they wisely declined to get involved. The situation remained unresolved, the Saudi government apprehensive and unwilling to confront the unknown. Thus stalemate set in. Eventually, again in the corporate language of today, the problem was kicked upstairs.

Reportedly, King Ibn Sa'ud himself came up with the answer: Let the Americans handle the problem. Let them "be the keeper at the gates" and assume the responsibility for the good behavior of those they allowed to visit his country. Surely Aramco would be most cautious in selecting and guaranteeing the conduct of such visitors, lest their actions, articles, and stories shame, criticize, or condemn the country's lifestyle. For, if the responsibility was abused, the concession agreement might be placed in jeopardy.

And so it came to be, with Aramco and the Saudi government entering into a strange new relationship that neither knew much about, a new management discipline that had been around for a number of years but which had seen its greatest growth and appli-

T.F. Walters, chief photographer.

cation during the postwar years. It was called public information, or public relations (PR) or, much later, communications. Public relations meant nothing more or less than relating to the public all of the positive information about a given company, its policies, and its products. It called for people who could, above all, write well, handle tough questions from all quarters, and build solid, positive, and enduring relationships with their prime targets: the editors, writers, and columnists of the nation's wire services, newspapers, magazines, and radio stations anywhere in the world. The world media, communicating primarily in Arabic and English—news hungry, independent, volatile, and political—would have to be identified, cultivated, and serviced with facts, news stories, features, and picture stories about Aramco and Saudi Arabia. Pitfalls aplenty for the unsophisticated, but a vital part of the communications process.

It was early 1946 and Aramco, headquartered at 225 Bush Street, San Francisco, did not have one man on the payroll who could handle this task. Nor did its personnel department know exactly what they should be looking for. As a result of an untimely heart attack suffered by a top executive, a desperate telephone call to Washington, D.C., and a tentative question posed by a board member of Socal, a person showed up at Aramco's offices who seemed just the sort of man who could do the job (whatever that might be).

The man hired to head up this new, nebulous function was a genuine hero of World War II whose credentials were truly awe inspiring. His was an extraordinary American success story, personifying all the qualities that one could ever hope to see in any young man. Skilled in the intricacies of government, a survivor of combat in various forms, and no stranger to foreign lands, it was clear that these experiences had made him an excellent candidate for any number of new, dangerous, or demanding assignments in post-World War II. His name was Howard Beir.

Howard was a 1938 graduate of the University of Pennsylvania, an ROTC second lieutenant who wound up as a reserve office, in the 16th Infantry Regiment, part of the 1st Division. Howard went to Washington, secured a job with the United States News (which subsequently became U.S. News & World Report, owned by David Lawrence), covered Senate hearings as well the White House, still fulfilling his reserve military obligations. In mid-1940 he went on active duty in the executive office of the president with an intelligence unit charged with intercepting the trans-shipment of war-related materials purchased from U.S. companies by South American organizations and subsequently sent to Germany. Beir, devising a simple system that put a stop to these sales, eventually became the executive secretary of the Export Control Policy Committee. He didn't much like his new boss, Henry Wallace, so he moved over to the War Production Board where an old friend, Edwin A. Locke, was an assistant to Donald Nelson, head of the WPA. Howard went off active duty and started to work with Locke.

Beir was in the right place to help people. Shortly after Japan declared war on the U.S., he got a call from a General Donovan, someone who he had once met years ago in Buffalo, New York. He knew Donovan was a great WWI hero and a prominent attorney. Now Donovan was heading up a new, covert organization called the Office of Strategic Services (OSS), but was frustrated by red tape that hindered his efforts to obtain such crucial items as explosives and short-range radios from suppliers that were shipping all their production to the armed forces. Beir, who had limited authority to approve priority applications, met Donovan, who told him what he needed. Back at his office, Howard assembled a 20-page list of the materials desperately sought by Donovan, filed an application and assigned an A-1A rating to it. Meeting Donovan again, he passed over the signed and dated license, but warned that in dealing with suppliers he was never to surrender the actual approval form, but to send them a telegram listing the A-1A rating and the license number. The general was skeptical but a few weeks later called to say that it was working with all suppliers. Donovan, in gratitude, said, "What can I do for you?" Howard said he wanted to see the war up real close and understood that Donovan's outfit might be flying people in and out of Occupied Europe on various missions.

Can you fly, he was asked. No, he answered. Within a week, Howard was in Alabama and 88 days later reported back to Washington with wings but no multiengine or instrument training. He then went to the Solomon Naval Training station in Maryland for a quick course in piloting Landing Craft, Personnel. Sent to Fort Benning, Georgia, he learned how to jump from a plane, earning his paratrooper wings in short order. Following a few days spent at a Canadian intelligence school, he flew to England, checked in with British paratroopers there and jumped with them enough times to qualify for his wings. Now a

Joe Alex Morris, writer.

Jack Mahoney, editor, Sun & Flare.

major, he was getting closer to the front lines, just what he was looking for.

He was assigned to RAF squadron #138, north of London, engaged in "special activities." Howard thought he was ready to fight the war. The British thought otherwise. Horrified at his minimal 200 hours of flying time and zero instrument flying ability, they took him under their wing, literally and figuratively. In time he was dropping agents into France, piloting a single-engined Lysander, flying on moonlit nights, now navigating on instruments. He flew about 35 such missions, with only a few close calls. Once the British signed off on him as trained and ready to move on, he was assigned to the OSS-Cairo team. But then he bumped into the territorial imperatives of the British secret services, which didn't want the OSS meddling in their affairs.

Chafing at the bit, Howard went off to see General Doolittle, who was just about to take over the 15th Army Air Force in Italy. He needed leaders and made Howard commander of the 514th Heavy Bombardment Squadron, one of four in the 376th Bomb Group, based at San Pancrazio. He flew more than 50 missions in B-24s, including 8 of the total of 13 missions that bombed the Ploesti oil fields in Rumania. At some point, somebody thought Howard was approaching burnout, so he was ordered back to the States to sell War Bonds. On one such a trip in Colorado, learning that the USAAF was assembling pilots to fly B-29s over Japan, he asked for a squadron, but was turned down. It was judged he already had enough combat duty and that there were too many young pilots eager for such assignments.

After five years, the war was over for Howard. He went on reserve status, just a few months shy of full colonel rank, ready to confront peacetime America. In early 1946, Howard was in San Francisco to take up an assignment as assistant to the president of the Pacific Can Company. But that man had a heart attack, decided to sell his company, and left Howard in the lurch. As luck had it, and with some assistance from Eddie Locke, the unemployed ex-flyer met a director of Socal, then another, who posed an unusual question to him: Would he go to Saudi Arabia to start up "some sort of a visitor-press liaison department," new to them. Howard said yes.

Within a couple of weeks, he had checked into Beit Aramco, Jiddah, and began working with Gary Owens, an attorney, and Winthrop Rockefeller, head of public relations for Texaco Oil Company, all of them reporting to Floyd Ohliger, vice president. Three months later, Howard was in Dhahran, setting up an office in the main administration building of Aramco, ready to ply his new trade. Dhahran, now with a new airbase built by the United States (and with the colossal growth of air travel), superseded Jiddah as the principal point of entry to Arabia. Dhahran was in Al Hasa Province, governed by Shaikh Abdullah Ibn Jiluwi, one of the men closest to King Ib'n Saud, and the governor of that province in which the oil operations were centered.

The first homes built are in the foreground with trees, foliage, and grass taking root. New homes (top) look a bit barren.

eir reported to Ohliger and did a good job. He welcomed various people to Arabia, got them settled into guest quarters, and, at that time, offered them a drink. Then he showed them around the field, as it was known, introducing them to an exploration team, getting them out to an oil drilling site in the desert, and impressing them with a huge, shiny, brand new refinery sitting on the shores of the Persian Gulf. Some of them dropped by the homes of American families living in Dhahran, Ras Tanura, or Abqaiq. Aramco's field management were accessible and made available plenty of statistics that powerfully impressed the visitors. Most got to see the local towns of Al Khobar, the fishing port of Dammam, and the thousand-year-old fort at Hofuf. Some special guests flew to visit Jiddah; a few were even invited to Riyadh.

Sami Kubassi, interpreter.

For the next two years, he handled the new assignment well. It culminated in the visit of David Douglas Duncan, the <u>Life</u> photographer, who for the first time extensively photographed the royal family. Indeed, the success of this assignment, managed to a considerable degree by Aramco, required Howard to return to the States.

By this time, Aramco had moved from San Francisco to 505 Park Avenue, Manhattan, where it took over the entire building. It now had a fully staffed public relations department with Harold O. "Tommy" Thompson as its vice president. Howard remained in New York, working on a variety of projects, including handling the visits of various members of the Saudi Royal Family. In 1952, he was invited to join Winthrop Rockefeller in a new venture to build subsidized housing for the masses in Iraq. The company was called IBEC, with offices at Rockefeller Center. Shortly after, Howard and his wife Amy (Ward), who worked for Aramco in its PR department, resigned from the company and left for a new life in Baghdad.

Tommy Thompson was a relatively new addition to the executive floors at 505 Park Avenue. (Prior to his arrival, J. T. Duce, a lawyer, was head of the government and public relations department.) The unusual fact that Aramco had created the post of vice president for the separate function of public relations seemed to testify to the growing importance of the function in light of developments in the Middle East.

Thompson was that rare individual who has made the segue from journalist to becoming a member of top management in one of America's newest and potentially highly profitable oil companies. As an outstanding newsman, he could think way beyond covering a story or meeting a deadline. As a long-time international correspondent with United Press, a prestigious wire service with hundreds of newspaper clients, he had served in many parts of the world, including China and Japan in the highly turbulent and dangerous thirties. As a young correspondent, he had followed the Japanese army as it entered Mukden in 1932 and filed numerous stories on the invasion of the Chinese mainland. He had served as bureau chief for the UPS Washington office. Based in Japan for several years, he had broken the story that Japan would join the Axis against the Allies. And as United Press bureau chief in Tokyo, he was one of the last newspapermen to be repatriated following Pearl Harbor.

Thompson, a rather beguiling man, was in his middle fifties when he joined Aramco. A New Yorker, he spoke softly and in unhurried flat tones, giving off a sense of calm and confidence. With a nice, deprecating sense of humor he chatted in a friendly, casual style with most people he met, and tended to ask questions (like any good journalist), which put them at ease as they provided answers. He also knew what he wanted and usually knew how to get it. Thompson was about to build an organization for the field and didn't have too much time to get it underway.

He was looking for two people to carry out specific functions in Arabia. First, he was looking for a suitable—but different—candidate to replace Howard. He found his man, a fellow newspaperman with impressive credentials, at the United Nations, who liked to write and felt there was no finer vocation. His name was Homer Metz.

Homer was the chief United Nations correspondent for the <u>Christian Science Monitor</u>, based in New York City (the UN was still in Long Island City, its own building not yet completed). He had worked on several major newspapers, including the <u>Pittsburgh Press</u> and the <u>Morning Telegraph</u> in New York City, covering several beats one of which was the Broadway theatre

Vern Tietjen and H.O. Thompson.

scene. His beat at the UN encompassed virtually every major development occurring there, particularly the volatility of the Middle East since the creation of Israel in 1948. He had been a little more than six years with the <u>Monitor</u>.

Recently divorced, he had just married Patricia Johnston, a press assistant in the office of Charles Malik, Lebanon's ambassador to the United Nations. Much younger than Homer, she was beautiful, sophisticated, and glamorous. Homer, in his early forties, handsome, with prematurely silver-graying hair, spoke in a cultivated voice, wrote well, knew lots of people in the news business and wielded influence there. He could also operate in business, diplomatic, and international spheres of activity. Too old for WWII, he had been responsible for the <u>Monitor's</u> daily front page update on the war.

Following a two-week indoctrination conducted at Aramco's Training Center, Riverhead, Long Island, Homer and Pat flew to Beirut, Lebanon, checking in at the St. George Hotel. Pat found an apartment on the Rue Corniche, as housing was not yet available in Dhahran. In a few days, Homer flew down there, was assigned bachelor quarters and went to work. He would be representing not only Aramco but its subsidiary, Tapline, which managed the thousand-mile long pipeline that stretched from Ras Tanura to Sidon, Lebanon, on the Mediterranean. Tapline, because of the volatile political situations that would soon arise, eventually became a full-time assignment, which would require that Homer relocate in Beirut, a development that suited him and Pat.

Immediately after Homer's appointment, Thompson found the second member of the management team he had been searching for. This time, Thompson selected a professional public relations executive, a new breed of manager with little if any journalistic experience, other than the fact that he could write exceedingly well and had worked closely with many editors, journalists, and columnists in media. He was a partner in a small public relations counseling firm which had its offices in Washington, D.C., and serviced a number of clients in and around that city. The firm, once retained by a client, analyzed its products or services, especially its unique values or problems, then created a marketing plan, a business strategy, and budget. Once approved, it executed the plan. The firm grew and prospered. Even so, W. Jack. Butler, 32, joined Aramco as assistant manager of public relations. Butler perhaps was looking for the adventure that had eluded him during his service as a lt. commander in the United States Navy; a night fighter carrier pilot, he never got to fight as the war ended while he was on his way to a combat assignment in the Pacific.

No doubt Thompson had advised him of the unique management structure that would await him upon his arrival in the field. Aramco, obviously, was a creature of its several owners, each one a major oil company. Each had a member on the Aramco board of directors, representing the special interests of that part-owner. The first head of the company was William F. Moore, who along with the heads of other departments, was based at 505 Park Avenue. Naturally, as New York City was the center of the media universe, public relations had to be based in Manhattan.

In the field, the top management was made up of several men who had been among the first to come ashore at Jubail and those who came later: Fred Davies, Floyd Ohliger, Tom Barger, to name just a few who rose to high rank and who spent almost all of their lives in Arabia. Of these, Floyd Ohliger served as vice president of government and public affairs, which included the newly established public relations function.

Ohliger was the front man who represented Aramco at Hofuf, Riyadh, Jiddah, and any where else King Ibn Sa'ud chose to have a meeting. A charming, affable man, he was backed by a first-class team of Arabists, Middle East experts, researchers, and interpreters, all headed up by Dr. George Rentz, a distinguished scholar with impressive academic credentials and a worldwide reputation; the interests of Aramco were in excellent hands. Nevertheless, public relations, as a new and somewhat dubious management tool, seemed to get the short end of the stick. Whereas the department had the task of generating and disseminating on a regular and continuing basis a wide variety of news throughout the world, in some quarters there was the feeling that such information did not serve the interests of either Aramco, and more particularly, the Saudi government. Thompson was convinced Butler could find

Leonard Turk, writer.

a way through the maze in the field.

Butler was another of those outstanding young men who had survived the war, a potential hero in the making, though doubly thwarted by circumstances. Home for him had been Port Huron, Michigan. He had attended the University of Michigan for two years, pursuing a degree in physics. A solid block of a fellow, he had played left tackle on Michigan's national championship team. Early in 1942 he entered the U.S. Navy and was sent to Pensacola, Florida, for flight training, eventually checking out on twin-engine Catalina sea planes. He was clearly combat-ready, itching to get into the war. He was ordered to the Phillipines, but the ship that was to transport him was interned by the Japanese. Then somebody thought he would be more valuable ferrying the top brass of the nation in and out of Washington, D.C., to numerous meetings involving congressmen, admirals, generals, and high-ranking civilians. So Jack was sent to American Airlines training school for six weeks to familiarize him with instrument flying on DC3s.

Jack's proven talents as a naval aviator, his specialized skills in navigation, plus a command presence that inspired confidence, definitely made him suitable for a career in the Navy. While keeping all of his passengers in one piece, Butler had a rare chance for a young man to observe the styles and conduct of many of the most important civilians in charge of the war. It was a frustrating situation. It was late 1944, the war in Europe was going well, with victory clearly in sight. But Japan was still going to be a tough nut to crack, everybody knew. Two years of chauffeuring was enough for him. He eventually won a reprieve, a chance to train as a night fighter pilot and to check out in landing aboard aircraft carriers.

The following month, the Enola Gay dropped the first atom bomb on Hiroshima, obliterating that city. Then the second one fell on Nagasaki, destroying it. Japan sued for peace. The war was over. For Jack, one last chance for a challenging adventure—though in peacetime—remained. A friend of his, Admiral William Byrd, had invited him to be a member of a scientific research team that would explore the South Pole. All that was needed was final approval by Congress to allocate funds for it. The project died for lack of them. After the war, Jack entered Harvard University where he earned a degree in physics, and later an MBA at the Harvard Business School.

When he joined Aramco, Tommy Thompson sent him to Dhahran, telling him to build a public relations organization to carry out a broad-gauge program that must be developed almost on the fly, de-

spite bumping into some of the convictions or concerns of others. Butler was going to have to build strong, cordial, and productive relationships with as many of the top field executives as possible. Reporting weekly to a top management review committee that dealt with a variety of immediate needs as well as future, long-term concerns, it was Butler's task to convince his audience of the merits of his proposals.

Butler made a powerful impression on nearly everyone he met. He was about six feet tall with a solid physique and stance that gave off an almost belligerent aura, topped off by handsome square features that matched the rest of him. He spoke in quiet, serious, measured tones that belied a subtle, ironic sense of humor, which was occasionally accompanied by an engaging half-smile. He was the antithesis of the standard publicity man people were beginning to bump into. He had weight, gravitas, for such a young man.

Fortunately for him, there were a few events bubbling away that would focus everyone's attention and gain him a measure of support from local management, albeit with the encouragement of the parent companies, whose take on world petroleum developments was a lot more knowledgeable than that of people in the field.

The first was the announcement in December of 1950 that Aramco and the Saudi Arabian government had agreed to a fifty-fifty split of profits from all of the oil operations carried out on behalf of Saudi Arabia, clearly the result of the 1948 fifty-fifty split between the Venezuelan government and the foreign oil companies operating in that country, which took almost six years to negotiate. This was a major revision of the original Aramco concession agreement and had taken many months of secret negotiations between both parties, all of which had to be considered in the context of the long-simmering disagreement between Iran and Britain, a majority stockholder in the Anglo-Iranian Oil Company. Muhammad Musaddiq, a powerful cleric, with strong ties to the communist Tudeh party, rejected the offer of a revised agreement.

Barely three months later, on March 7, 1951, Iran's Prime Minister Razmara was assassinated and a week later, on March 15, the Iranian Majlis voted to nationalize the oil industry, a decision that was ratified by the Iranian Senate the following week. Musaddiq became prime minister of Iran on April 29, 1951. The world's oil industry, including Aramco and its owners, took stock of this extraordinary development and waited apprehensively. Winston Churchill, back in power, threatened war.

Musaddiq had a good case, much of the world thought. The British, it was well known, exercised far too much influence on the country, aided and abetted by its ruler, Reza Shah Pahlavi. Iran at that time was the fourth largest oil producer in the world, with even more immense reserves of natural gas. Only a tiny fraction of the wealth generated by oil seeped down to its 15 million people, only a few of whom were employed by AIOC, a deliberate policy of Britain for many years. The Saudi government was not going to tolerate any such restraints, and continued to press Aramco to push forward the education of the Saudi employees.

Understandably, the owner companies of Aramco were worried about the possibility that nationalization of the Iranian oil industry might adversely affect the position of Aramco. Hence, they were determined to improve their public relations position in Saudi Arabia and the entire Middle East.

With such new momentum on his side, Butler scrambled around looking for people already in the field who could fit some of the job descriptions he had developed: a visitor relations man, who could handle the increasing number of visitors to the field, which included U.S. government officials, heavy hitters from the parent companies, the growing cadre of journalists, writers, and photographers who wanted to visit and document the extraordinary story of this ancient, long-forgotten desert kingdom

Sayeed, driver.

A first class photo-journalist was discovered working in the engineering department in Abqaiq. Thomas F. Walters, who had served in the 15th Army Air Force as a navigator/bombardier had completed 35 missions in B-24s, mostly over Germany. He had been encouraged to join Aramco by his mother and step-father, already working in Ras Tanura, Arabia. He transferred to Dhahran, started shooting news, documentary, and picture stories to illustrate stories being written by Homer Metz, as well as servicing journalists visiting the field who needed pictures to support their articles. It wasn't long before Walters recommended that the department construct its own photo-lab to meet the increasing requests for copies of pictures he had taken. This project, quickly approved and under construction, sent him looking for a photo-lab technician to help run it. He found a likely candidate doing the same sort of work for the exploration department, invited the

young man to join the PR department and then moved him into the new lab, where he eventually developed into a capable backup photographer to Walters.

Ever since he had arrived in Dhahran, Butler had been working closely with Graham Associates, an independent graphic design group established by Roy and Ray Graham, twin brothers. With impressive links to the original CASOC, and then Aramco, they had carried out a number of important assignments, including the production of the first employee handbooks, as well as producing the original inhouse company magazine and other materials. Later they got into the production of several educational films, which addressed the health issues of the Saudis. Butler liked them because they were incredibly resourceful, could handle virtually any challenge thrown at them, and always delivered a first-class product. Ray and Jack had frequently discussed the long-range goals of the public relations department, including more films, among them a feature length movie on the creation of Saudi Arabia by Ibn Sa'ud. Butler also wanted to get underway a book about the first explorers of Arabia; he even had an author for it: Wallace Stegner, a very successful author whose writing he enjoyed, someone he felt who could extract the best from what was already a great adventure story.

Abdullah Tariki and W. Jack Butler.

Things were beginning to take shape.

The oil operations in the early fifties were booming, with the greatest period of growth well underway in Aramco's short life. The three principal towns that controlled oil operations, Dhahran, Ras Tanura, and Abqaiq, were rapidly expanding to accommodate the growing influx of people, and to provide new and additional services for them. Twice a week Aramco's two DC-4s—the Camel and the Gazelle—landed at Dhahran's airport full of talented men and women hired to fill new jobs, or to serve as replacements for those going on a so-called long vacation, or for those who couldn't cut it for one reason or another. Sometimes people made the decision themselves, acknowledging that they were overwhelmed by the immensity of the desert, the boiling heat of the sun, or the challenges of working with a half-dozen different nationalities: Saudis, Indians, Pakastanis, Palestinians, Dutch, Italians, and even their fellow Americans. Sometimes Aramco made the decision for them. There

were no recriminations, no penalties. Just climb aboard the plane and head for home.

Meanwhile, back in New York, Thompson began sending out a number of young men to help meet the growing need to generate copy for all sorts of end uses: booklets and brochures; articles for the Aramco World, a once-small house organ that was expanding each year; copy that would be used in material sent to schools throughout the United States; reporters for the Sun & Flare, the weekly newspaper produced in Dhahran and distributed to all employees in the field. Also, there were plans afoot to create an Arabic language magazine, to be directed at all Saudi employees.

It seems that Thompson was partial to the Ivy League, recruiting newly graduated young men with BA degrees. One was Joe Alex Morris, Jr., a Harvard graduate who had served as an intern general assignment reporter at the Minneapolis Star, a major daily. He was the son of Joe Alex Morris, who'd worked for the United Press, was once an editor of the Saturday Evening Post, and had written several books. Joe Jr. completed his two-year contract with Aramco, then moved on to become the Middle East correspondent for Newsweek and its parent, the Los Angeles Times.

Other young men included Al Iardella, a graduate of Columbia University; and Francois Lachelier, a Frenchman, graduate of Yale. The idea, perhaps, was to catch them before being corrupted by the business world or political influences inimical to the tasks at

Tom Gartland, editor.

hand. Later on, William Scott, an instructor in English and journalism at the American University of Beirut, Lebanon, was quickly recruited by Butler. Paul West, a somewhat older writer who had spent several years in Latin America, came on board but did not stay beyond one contract. Finally, a mature newspaperman, Vern Tietgen , recommended to Thompson by a golfing friend, turned out to be a competent wordsmith (a sports writer by trade, as he put it), who could cover anything that came over the transom. He spent the next dozen years in Dhahran and Beirut covering the needs of both Aramco and Tapline, before retiring to The Dalles in Oregon. He played tennis, too.

In 1952, as a result of the process of change and evolution that the Saudi government was constantly seeking, Aramco moved its corporate headquarters from New York to Dhahran. This also necessitated that most of the principal officers of the corporation (with the exception of public relations) had to take up residence in the field. Some changes in top management came about, such as the arrival of Robert L. Keyes in April of that year, brought in from Texaco to become president. Fred A. Davies became chairman of the board. Later on Norman Cy Hardy joined Aramco as executive vice president. Robert I. Brougham, originally based in New York, came to the field and became senior vice president of finance.

Al Iardella, writer.

Brougham was an avid tennis player, who on previous visits to the field had discovered that Butler was a worthy adversary, which resulted in a relationship that proved mutually beneficial on a number of occasions. Keyes, another tennis buff, along with Bill Owen, the company's senior lawyer, joined them, which made for some pretty challenging matches on the Dhahran courts. Bill Taylor, a surgeon at Dhahran's brand new medical center, was another tennis devotee, a good man to have on your side of the net in doubles.

Now, where at one time most of the major decision-making processes had been lodged seven thousand miles away in Manhattan, they were just down the hall in various offices contained in the new administration building at Dhahran. This move improved various efficiencies at almost every level of the executive branch, which made sense to Aramco, its parent company owners, and especially the Saudi government, which had pressed for this action. For Aramco was growing larger by the day, hiring more people to do highly specialized jobs, expanding its training capabilities to bring more young, capable Saudis into the work force. More and

larger oilfields were being discovered, placed into production, and shipped as crude oil or refined products into world markets. The parent companies that owned Aramco now had several of their own people on site, which was reassuring.

On August 19, 1952, Jack Butler and his wife Pat went on a well-earned long vacation, leaving Michael Cheney in charge as acting manager of the public relations department. That same day President Mohammed Mossadegh of Iran was toppled by a public uprising, an event in which the CIA played an important—and controversial—role. Saudi Arabia, on the surface remained calm and Aramco went about its daily business. Other major political events during the remaining part of that year and in the following year did little to destabilize the oil operations, despite the fact that a couple of them were getting close to home. The king was responding to growing signs of incipient nationalism.

The all-important thing to keep in mind was that despite the rumors that King Ibn Sa'ud was in declining health, he was still very much in charge of the country. His word was inviolate, the impact of the growing oil royalties on the daily activities of the government beneficial and substantial. In his earlier years of conquest and consolidation, he had secured power in numerous ways, some of them cruel and bloodthirsty, by all other standards. Money had always been a bit of a challenge. It was no more.

Putting money and power together added immeasurably to that power. His exercise of it in subsequent years was masterful, worthy of comparison with other great personalities in history and contemporaneous times. He could and did meet with the great public figures, matching them in his perception of the moment, its significance to him, and above all, displaying his convictions that rarely yielded more than he was prepared to yield. He had a stable of counselors, many of them citizens of the surrounding countries, whose presence he required at the daily court he conducted in Riyadh. He listened to them, weighed the value of that advice and its consequences, and rendered his judgement. He was wily, he was cautious, he was absolute.

*****

Butler returned sometime in the fall after having spent some additional time at Harvard, completing degree requirements for an MBA. He returned with a good idea of what he thought he would be able to accomplish in his second contract. A week in the

New York office, conferring with H.O. Thompson on the future public relations goals of the company, had been satisfying. There was general agreement between them that the department had been successful in the limited programs currently being carried out. The external elements of it—reaching out to the world of media in whatever form required—was working reasonably well. Journalists from across the world were spending more time on the Middle East and its numerous and complicated religious, political, and economic issues. Inevitably, Saudi Arabia was part of that turbulent area, yet without any overt turbulence of its own. Its government was perceived as being stable with no internal dissent at the palace level, and nothing of any consequence with its tribal affiliations or life in the towns and villages of Arabia. As for Aramco, its relations with the government were sound, the company doing its job, though not always as aggressively as was demanded by an impatient partner. Fortunately the royalties were increasing monthly, the prospects for that continuing better than ever. No doubt the management of Aramco on site, and the top executives of the parent companies in the States, felt that their huge investments in a Saudi Arabia ruled by King Sa'ud were sound and secure. But everybody knew that he was going to be a very tough act to follow.

William A. Scott, assistant manager, P.R. department.

The advent of television was reviewed. It was going to have a tremendous impact on those parts of the world that could understand, afford, permit—and exploit it. Its introduction in America during 1948 was a case in point. About 1.5 million black-and-white sets had been bought in one year, 15 million the next. As Thompson and Butler agreed, entertainment was one thing, but the potential for its application for education vastly more intriguing. It was visual, immediately understood by all.

Still pictures were yet a major part of the outreach communications effort, and a number of short, health-medical motion pictures were being produced in the field to educate the Saudis about the need to understand and eliminate such diseases as trachoma.

These films were usually shown in a number of the small villages, a 16mm projector rigged on a flatbed truck, with power supplied by a portable generator. When night fell, the truck backed up to a convenient wall, the noise of the generator attracting the curious villagers who gathered about the truck to see what was going on.

For many it was their first movie, which generated an excited buzz as the screen lit up. Once the sound and action began to take place, the villagers went silent, sat down on the ground, becoming totally absorbed in what the narrator was saying. Only the police were walking about, flicking their canes at women who were attempting to view the film under cover of the darkness. The reach and impact that television could have by utilizing materials already produced could be incalculable as an educational tool on the population, if accepted by the religious and government.

The July-August 1953 issue of the Harvard Business Review carried an article entitled "Public Relations for Industry in Undeveloped Countries," written by W. Jack Butler. The 3,500-word piece spelled out the new role that American businesses must play throughout the world "if it wanted to continue their operations abroad." It was a comprehensive piece that identified more than a dozen elements that U.S. companies were usually reluctant to address—or were ignorant of the fact that they existed and needed to be addressed. Few companies sensed that they had to drastically rethink how to operate in the new world, to play a role far different from the minor one—largely philanthropic— played in earlier generations and other regions.

As Butler pointed out, American had been known "only as educators and founders of agricultural and medical missions," these efforts had been gratefully accepted by small and impoverished nations with the understanding that there would be no tampering with the fundamentals of the country: the rulers, government, religion, custom, and other inhibitors sanctified by time and tradition.

He cautioned that things would have to change on both sides of the equation. If American industry wanted to be a player in these new

King Sa'ud and Pat Butler.

T. F. Walters

international undertakings—and profit accordingly—it would have to change. If the lands faraway wanted to prosper from what U.S. companies appeared to be offering, they too would have to yield, somewhat.

The piece addressed several problems that industry management would face as it sought to export and exploit America's unique national characteristics—optimism, energy, imagination—fueled by a scale of industrial capacity that beggared description. The list of challenges was long: the utilization of caption and the essentiality of profit, political sensitivities, social change, xenophobia, the training of men (and women) for roles in an industrial environment for which they had little comprehension.

Add to these long-entrenched governments, ruling classes gripped by avarice (even fear), the general population suffused with general bewilderment (and fear, too). And not least, it was imperative that American instructors, supervisors, and employees temper their zeal to better understand their new employees hemmed in by archaic traditions, religious beliefs, and cultural patterns almost inviolate.

Butler cited examples from South America (including oil companies), the Middle East, and Saudi Arabia, to support his charge that much more had to be done. He singled out the Arabian American Oil Company (Aramco) as a litmus test of much that was good. Just what sort of circulation the HBR received in the field was unknown, or whether the author needed prior authorization to write such a piece is also unknown. It was a singular article for the times, a gutsy piece that needed telling.

A new and major undertaking of the public relations department was a film that would encompass the consolidation of Arabia by Ibn Sa'ud, up to that point the emir of the Nejd. A so-called feature in the best traditions of movie-making (although not Hollywood), it was an ambitious project that would also span the history and culture of the Arabs, culminating in the capture of Riyadh by Sa'ud and a small band of men. This event signaled the rise of the House of Sa'ud, whereupon he became the king of Saudi Arabia, and keeper of the holy places, Mecca and Medina.

The film would have a quality of content and production values that was expected to secure for it broad distribution, especially in those parts of the world where the Moslem faith was practiced. Ray Graham Associates was retained, along with Lyford Associates, to develop a script and in due time assemble a crew to produce the film, which would have many shooting locations in Arabia and other parts of the world. A major production compared with the numerous single subject medical- and health-related films previously produced, this feature called for close government scrutiny, final approval, and a hefty budget. The script was approved by Riyadh, with Aramco agreeing to pick up the tab. Its working title: The Island Of Allah. Production got underway. It would take two years to complete.

In late 1953, the rumors that Ibn Sa'ud was near death were confirmed. The doughty old warrior, whose age was calculated to be about 84, died in November at Tayif, his summer residence. He was promptly buried in an unmarked grave outside Riyadh, his body pointing towards Mecca, as custom prescribed. His son, Crown Prince Sa'ud, selected 20 years before by his father and whose most important function had been to maintain strong ties to the principal Bedouin tribes, was immediately proclaimed king.

The world waited, not knowing if this would meet with the approval of the royal family and the government (one and the same), and all others who had sworn allegiance to Ibn Sa'ud. Aramco's government relations department, on the scene and with a somewhat better sense of the moment, felt that the succession would proceed as ordained. And so it was, the House of Sa'ud continued, the new king making a sweep in early 1954 thorough the principal portions of his kingdom, especially Al Hasa. Here he would visit with its governor, Sheik Abd Allah Ibn Jiluwi, cousin of the late King, at Hofuf. He would also spend a few days at Dhahran, center of the oil operations. (See "Portraits: Royal Family", page 68.)

Those nations who were large consumers of Arabian crude had begun to count on Saudi Arabia as a reliable source of oil ("Arabian Sweet"), were further relieved at the aggressive exploration and drilling programs that revealed vast new fields, such as Air Dar, Ghawar, Uthmania, Haradh, and the first offshore drilling site at Safiniya, in the northeast corner of Arabia. Such good news and confirmation of a stable government for the foreseeable future earned for Aramco and the Saudi government the growing respect of the oil-dependent world. (Allah Akbar!)

As a result of these new discoveries, more and more Americans (and the first trickle of Europeans) were being recruited and arriving in the field twice a week on the company planes. As Aramco's field guide reported, the period between 1949 and 1955 reflected the largest number of Americans, and also the largest number of Saudis who joined the company. The Americans were mature, experienced people whose talents covered the full spectrum of industrial needs; the Saudis were much younger, with few if any perceived talents. (Improved aptitude tests and other systems especially designed to identify talents were now able to estimate the inherent or innate values of the newly-recruited Saudis.)

Their recruitment permitted the advancement of those who had been filling entry-level positions and were now sufficiently skilled to move up the ladder into new tasks or assignments. The relatively rapid rise of these young people based on performance alone (unencumbered by historic or traditional lengthy apprentice programs) made a good impression on them. These good impressions traveled to other towns and villages and recruitment became somewhat easier, with more candidates showing up for employment. The possibility that a job with good pay, better food, medical benefits, and, eventually, home ownership was clearly the work of Allah. Most soon learned to show up for work every day.

As the world began to pay more attention to Aramco on a more frequent and even continuing basis, so more interest was being shown in what impact the ever-increasing royalties pouring into the Saudi treasury were having on the king, the royal family and the government. Just when the term "conspicuous consumption" came into common usage is not clear, but it did not have to exist for the condition to prevail. Granted, the government established programs covering education, medical facilities, housing, and

P.R. department, Dhahran.

many other public services—again, that great word infrastructure comes to mind—that Arabia, which had had virtually none before, needed now. But its bureaucracy was meager, with little independent authority to set priorities, establish budgets, or manage the incredible number of projects that were initiated or approved by the King. There were a few critics. One, H St. John B. Philby, still in residence (the home given to him by Ibn Sa'ud many years before) in Riyadh, was aghast at the profligate conduct of the principals in Riyadh. He castigated them in print, speeches, and in his several books. One, Golden Jubilee, published in 1952, was a paen to the virtues of the late king, whose legacy Philby saw being destroyed by the royal family. And the travels, antics, and general behavior of a number of young princes traveling far beyond the confines of Jiddah, Riyadh, and even Beirut and Cairo, generated news stories that soon got back to Riyadh to the displeasure of many, especially

the religious. Fortunately, Aramco could not be held responsible for such behavior.

In the early part of 1953, Butler hired William A. Scott to join the department. At the time Scott was a faculty member at the American University of Beirut (AUB), Beirut, where he taught journalism and also supervised the production of the campus newspaper. He had been hired to write a freelance piece on six young Saudis who had just arrived on campus to begin their undergraduate work. An Aramco photographer worked with Bill to provide pix to illustrate the article. (See "AUB: The Gamble", page 88.) Butler liked Scott (who had earned a BA in languages and literature from Kansas State and an MA in English from the University of Arizona) and invited him to join Aramco. He joined the department in Dhahran shortly after that and over time managed many of the divisions, ultimately becoming head of the department in 1961.

For some time, Butler had been reporting on a weekly basis to Aramco's top management, which included several board members, newcomers since Aramco moved its headquarters to Dhahran. These executives had a much broader range of management expertise as most were representing parent companies, owners of Aramco. Nevertheless the experience, insights, and sensitivities of such men as Davies, Ohliger, Eeds, Barger, and other pioneers, were invaluable, especially in the eyes of Riyadh, very much a partner.

A special project that intimately involved a number of these early explorers was moving along reasonably well. Earlier Butler had proposed that a book be written about their early experiences, preferably by a distinguished outsider, one sufficiently gifted who could dig out the story and provide the objectivity needed for acceptance by the literate world. He had someone in mind, the novelist Wallace Stegner, whose novel, Angel of Repose, had won a Pulitzer Prize. Contacted by Butler, Stegner accepted the assignment and began to work on it, visiting the field on several occasions to interview many of the principals, conducting the research along the way. The book had the working title, *Discovery!* It was completed in 1968, but for a variety of reasons, its publication by Middle East Export Press, Beirut, was delayed until 1971. Nevertheless, it was universally approved and is still considered the best and most dramatic telling of the early days of exploration and the men who made it all possible.

But the greatest undertaking of the department was the introduction of Aramco Television, begun in 1956. This task had been assigned to Bill Scott, who managed it from day one, going on the air in September of the following year, the first ever television broadcasting system introduced in the Middle East, let alone the kingdom. Its content was comprehensive: news, many popular U.S. television shows (censored for content), educational, films, and what might today be called public service information. It was eagerly accepted by employees, closely monitored by the government, and clearly met a pent-up demand for information and entertainment (but did not put the weekly newspaper, the <u>Arabian Sun</u>, out of business).

In late fall, Butler was advised that the king, who had been cutting a swath through the Middle East, as well as visiting a number of European countries, planned on accepting an invitation to speak before the UN General Assembly in New York. It would be his first visit to the United States as a head of state. It was natural to assume that he would be invited to Washington and the White House, to meet with President Harry S Truman. His reception by the general citizenry (including a large Jewish community) of New York City might be a bit dicey, although the rest of the nation was largely unperturbed. The public relations department was asked to make recommendations for this trip in light of its complexity, possible pitfalls, and duration, with the king traveling with a large retinue. This would be the first time that the department would be working cheek-by-jowl with the equivalent organization in the Royal Family, headed up by Shaikh Abdullah Bulkhair, presumably still functioning as the king's private secretary. Bulkhair hit it off with Butler and invited him to plan and manage the entire affair, accompanying the king's entourage.

By this time the department was running smoothly, its various sections well-staffed and even more cosmopolitan than before. Michael Cheney had resigned and intimated to a couple of people that he was thinking of a writing career, perhaps even a book of some sort. First, though, he and his family were going to spend a year

in England, to unwind and smell the roses. Vern Tietgen moved to Beirut with his wife, serving the interests of Tapline, reporting to Homer Metz. (See "A Half Century", page 14.)

On January 20, 1957, Butler boarded the SS <u>Constitution</u>, then docked in Naples, joining King Sa'ud's entourage, which numbered 40. No wives accompanied him, but he had brought along a young son who was afflicted with infantile paralysis. The boy was going to be examined by specialists in the States to determine treatment and, hopefully, a cure. Butler and Bulkhair spent their time aboard ship fine-tuning the numerous details of the trip. A number of photographs were taken of various people, including some of King Sa'ud with the young invalid. Upon reaching Gibralter, Butler debarked and boarded a plane to New York, meeting with H.O. "Tommy" Thompson, Aramco's vice president of public relations in the company's offices at 505 Park Avenue. A selection of several prints were offered to the *New York Times*. The day the SS <u>Constitution</u> docked, a picture of the King and his son appeared on its front page. As usual, a number of other national and regional newspapers noted this coverage and in various ways began to cover the visit of King Sa'ud to America. It was, altogether, a mixed bag, with New York's tabloid press offering giant headlines, as expected. The Washington reception went exceedingly well, with the red carpet rolled out at every venue. All in all, it was a successful, well-managed tour, which pleased the Saudi government. Butler spent a few days in the New York office, conferred with various members of the P.R. department, then boarded the <u>Camel</u> on its regularly scheduled eastward trip to Dhahran. He went back to work the next day.

Aramco Management in T.V. Studio.

Showtime! Lyford Productions had completed the feature film, <u>Jazirat Al Arab</u>, and, following a few minor changes, it was ready for distribution. Prints were ordered, a premier showing was planned, and the kickoff taking place in Cairo, another in Alexandria. Personalities of all sorts were invited (including a couple of exotic Italian film stars), the featured players, of course, and a selection of Aramco representatives and Saudi government officials.

It was 1955. It was the last year of five that reflected the great annual growth of employees, which from this point on it began to stabilize and soon decline. The discovery of new wells continued; the production of oil from these new and existing oil fields grew to a new, daily level of 965,041 barrels, this product quickly absorbed by the world oil markets. Royalties accrued to the treasury of Saudi Arabia at an ever increasing rate, but even so, there was more outgo than income. Aramco was obliged to advance considerable sums to the government to fund a number of ambitious projects conceived by the king and members of his immediate family. Quite often these projects, initially entered into by Riyadh, were supervised by Aramco. The natural growth of the royal family, and the generosity of King Sa'ud to officials and many of these young princes, raised concerns, which became more public over time. Yet the government was stable and remained so, despite the growing grumblings in certain quarters.

The king's visit to America had been a public relations success, despite him being picketed at UN headquarters, as well at the Waldorf-Astoria, where he was staying. Being ignored by the mayor of New York and vilified in the tabloid press was understood by King Sa'ud, who was fast becoming a sophisticated world traveler. Butler's management of many aspects of this trip brought him into close contact with several members of the "cabinet" especially

Shaikh Abdullah Tariki, first head of the oil operations. Heretofore, all direct contacts with His Majesty and his counselors had been led by Floyd Ohliger, a pattern that had been early established in the 1930s with King Ibn Sa'ud, and continued with the ascension of his son to the throne in 1953. On occasion, this direct access to certain people that Butler had earned proved to be of value as public relations as a management tool became better understood by Aramco and the Saudi government. Such access gave him insights into a closely guarded environment and much to think about.

As a result of these and other developments in late July of 1957, Butler set in motion an ambitious project for the consideration of Aramco. In a confidential memo addressed to R.A. Eeds, vice president of industrial relations (with a copy to H.O. Thompson), Butler proposed that Dr. Arnold Toynbee, the world's leading historian, be retained to carry out a study.

Butler felt that Dr. Toynbee should be asked to look into the future on a number of specific subjects that could be addressed by the distinguished historian in light of not only his grasp of world history, but also because of his special understanding of the Middle East. It was a field in which America and Aramco were still woefully ignorant. This proposal was vetted by various members of management and approved. In the following month, Butler met with Dr. Toynbee in Beirut, who reacted positively to the proposal and agreed to it. A fee was agreed upon, and in late August a contract was prepared by H.O. Thompson, with Butler stipulated as the coordinator, and submitted to Dr. Toynbee. He signed it on September 18, 1957.

In February of 1960, Butler submitted his resignation to Aramco. He was 40 years old and had spent almost ten years in the field. As assistant manager of the public relations department when he arrived in 1949, he developed a nucleus of communications specialists: an editor, a newspaper layout man, two writers, a pair of translators and interpreters, a couple of photographers, a secre-

Aramco management (left to right): "Spike" Spurlock, Tom Barger, Fred A. Davies, Norman Hardy, Bill Burleigh, Roy Lebkicher, Dick Bramkamp.

tary, and a driver (with a depth perception problem). By 1959, as manager, his department had expanded to more than 97 men and women, professionals in all the communications specialties. From this point on, as far as he was concerned, all it needed was a competent administrator to manage the department. (He couldn't take any direct credit for it, but it just so happened that in every year of his affiliation with Aramco, crude oil production increased. In 1949, it was 476,736 barrels a day—in 1959, it was 1,095,399 barrels. Today, in 2005, it is running around six of seven million barrels.)

Besides, he wanted to move on, into other fields with broader management responsibilities, greater rewards. He could see none of this happening with Aramco in Arabia and was aware that there was not much chance of a transfer to any one of the parent companies, which observed the no-poaching rule in their search for good people. Even so, he received some very attractive offers from Texaco, Exxon, and Mobil, shortly after he and his family returned to New York (so much for proselytizing). After a good look at several opportunities outside the industry, several of which were financially quite attractive, he accepted an offer to join Mobil Oil Company in its public relations department.

_____

Within a year Jack Butler had broken out of that narrow, somewhat restrictive assignment, moving to London to head up Mobil's public relations, industrial relations, and government relations functions, as part of the corporation's decision to decentralize its worldwide operations. During the next dozen or so years, Butler and his family resided in Copenhagen, Paris, London, and New York, from which at different times as managing director, he managed a number of European affiliates of Mobil. He subsequently moved into the African and Middle Eastern operation of the company, with more than 20 marketing units reporting to him, including Aden, which placed him once again on the Arabian mainland (where he negotiated a joint venture with the Ali Reza family, and another with Jiddah-Saudi Arabia). Butler was in the dead center of Mobil Oil Company's worldwide marketing of its petroleum and petroleum by-products.

The Arab-Israeli War of 1973 changed all that.

In 1974, Mobil Oil Company directed Butler to establish Mobil Saudi Arabia and appointed him as chairman of the board. (Mobil sought much greater involvement in the Middle East, with greater access to more of that Arabian crude.) The parent company instructed him to establish his headquarters in Saudi Arabia, with three objectives: the building of a new 657-mile-long pipeline from Jubail in Al Hasa province to the port of Yenbo on the Red Sea; the construction of a huge new refinery; and, finally, to design and manage the construction of a giant petrochemical plant that would throw off the numerous by-products from oil. The estimated cost of these three projects was about $10 billion. Butler was clearly the only man who could show up in Arabia and make things happen. He was, finally, in the catbird seat.

A couple of months later that same year, he and his wife Pat returned to Saudi Arabia, making their home in Jiddah. He immedi-

New homes, spindly bushes, and grass just about ready for mowing were all signs of new people, increased oil production, and great royalties.

*ately began to renew his social, business, and government relation-
ships formed during his nearly ten year stint with Aramco. Exactly
ten years later—in 1984—he announced his retirement, the three
enormous tasks assigned him (plus some others that cropped up
along the way) completed, or nearly so. They had been conducted
on time and within budget. Butler was asked by Mobil Oil Company to continue serving it as a consultant. He and his wife currently
make their home in Manhattan. He didn't wind up in the front lines
during World War II, nor did he get to the South Pole with Admiral
Robert Byrd, but had to settle for a tough—but exhilarating—35-
year, world-wide career in communications, advertising, marketing, and management.*

Allah Akbar! (God is Great!)

Portraits: The Americans

Obviously there were other foreign nationals working and living in Arabia during those early days following World War II, but the predominance of U.S. citizens was clear—and would remain so for many years to come.

Fortunately, over time Aramco had access to resourceful people in Western Europe and other parts of the Middle East who served the company well as it struggled to recruit and train Saudis for entry level and advanced positions in the oil company. Among the first to show up were the Italians, from Eritrea and Italian Somaliland. They were skilled craftsmen, construction stiffs, some very proficient in stonework.

Unfortunately, early in the war, the Italian air force set out to bomb the oil facilities of Bapco on Bahrain Island. The bombs fell in error on Saudi Arabia, doing little damage, but King Ibn Sa'ud was quite upset and apparently declared that Italian employees hired by Aramco would be denied living conditions comparable to the Americans. The Italians shrugged and created a lifestyle of their own (including an Italian

Charlie Bevin, District Manager, personified the spirit of Abqaiq.

restaurant at Al Aziziyah, which offered good food and a beachfront ambience for the Americans). At Ras Tanura, Ilo the Pirate, another Italian entrepreneur, became a free-lance photographer, and profited accordingly.

The creation of the state of Israel in 1947 brought about the exodus of hundreds of thousands of Palestinians from Palestine, providing an enormous pool of sophisticated and educated men from which Aramco could recruit people with special professional and business skills. It did so.

The world's economy that created hard and soft currencies in the fifties significantly affected the marketing strategies of the oil industry's products. Aramco (no doubt encouraged by its owners), established the Aramco Overseas Corporation (AOC) in Holland in order to spend those soft currencies on many items needed in Arabia, such as foodstuffs, Drambui, Tuborg, and many other items. Before long, professional men and women were being recruited for posts in all three districts, especially in the field of medicine; doctors,

medical technicians, and nurses, staffing the needs of the facilities in each area.

Aramco, almost by accident, was fast becoming an international society. It was a most agreeable development, most people thought. The Americans invited everyone to join in their off-hours lifestyles, which included virtually every sport imaginable: golf, tennis, basketball, football, etc. The Dutch established a fencing group, which was quite popular. Football (or soccer) appealed to a number of Saudis and Palestinians, albeit organized by a Lebanese American. A horse farm was established pretty quickly. Philately, photography, and other hobbies were a given. Book clubs, discussion groups, canasta and bridge clubs effortlessly came into being.

However you looked at it, it was pretty much a reflection of what was going on back home, in small town America. Stable, confident people with talents and skills and—above all else—an attitude that was generous and forgiving. If you didn't have that, it wasn't worth staying. The rest of the world had little idea of what was going on in this desert country of Bedouins, camels, and oil.

Hey, that was O.K. by the Aramcons.

Charlie Miller, Personnel, Dhahran.

A nurse at the Dhahran health center.

Talented artists produced exceptional paintings of local scenes.

Bill Reilly, principal of Dhahran High School.

The dining hall In Dhahran was the center of life for the community, especially for bachelors and bachelorettes who had the option of getting three meals a day here, if they so desired. Counter service was convenient and reasonably quick for late risers. A sit-down dining area was available in the rear, which could readily be modified for a banquet or large meeting room. The food was pretty good, too.

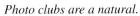
Authenticity: A play-by-play announcer

Photo clubs are a natural.

Bill Taylor receives trophy at Tennis Club Awards Dinner.

Maegie Scott, government relations (and tennis player).

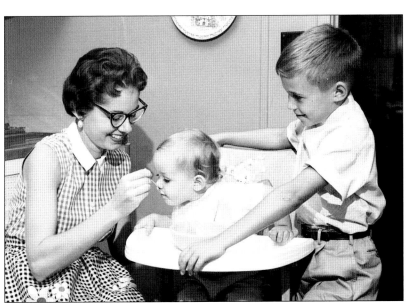

Kakki Kearney feeds Stephen, 1, while James, 8, assists.

Dhahran's library wasn't big, so it was always busy.

43

Football was just for the young guys, they said.

Secretaries, a vital part of any business, met the Aramco challenge all the way.

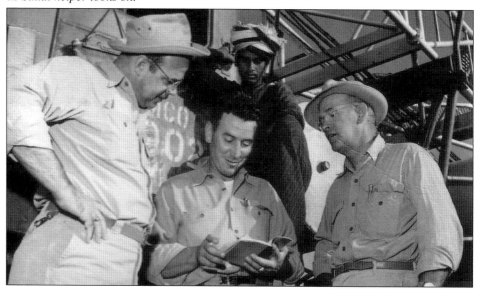

Art Pearsall with fellow workers at Dhahran heavy equipment yard, as Saudi helper looks on.

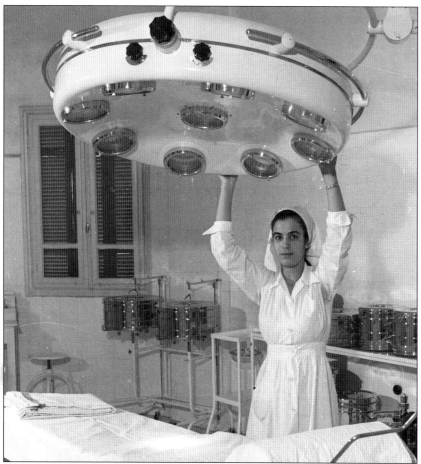

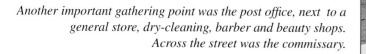

Nurse in operating room.

Another important gathering point was the post office, next to a general store, dry-cleaning, barber and beauty shops. Across the street was the commissary.

No slam dunks here.

Fashion shows were fun, with the search for exotic materials in the local suqs often rewarding as merchants imported more choices from Beirut and other sources.

Employees received Aramco service pins as one more measure of loyalty.

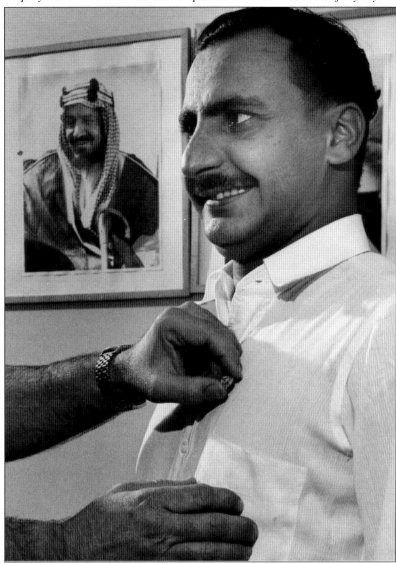

'Gip' Oldham and 'Cappy' Lock, Aramco pilots with a visitor and son in front of their DC-3, part of the company's air fleet. This was taken at Tapline's Quaisumah Pumping Station in 1951.

The judge and parents seem to be getting a bigger kick out of this event than the young man, the creator/operator of this prize winning vehicle.

Meetings, and more meetings.

Ras Tanura made sailors of many people, what with the blue Persian Gulf beckoning and the possibility of a cooling breeze to go with it.

Uthmaniyah, one of the more remote outposts, completed in 1954.

Good tailors at Al Khobar.

Luncheon of Dhahran's Women's Club at Dining Hall.

Future geologist, daughter of Aramcon employee.

Ray Malinowski, avid golfer, waits on the elevated par 3 tee for the green to clear.

Another golf course, of course.

It wasn't long before a horse farm came into being, on the Dhahran-Al Khobar Road. Most any animals were welcome.

Players and cheerleaders.

Safety pin-up girl.

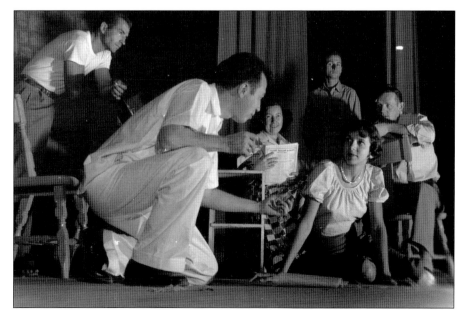

Jack Kibbee, son of famous Hollywood director, does the same thing in Dhahran, producing/directing many plays.

Shoppers meet a young member of the Hofuf community, right.

Dan Gallagher conducts a little practice session with the Dhahran junior softball team.

The King is Dead, Long Live…

For the first time ever in the brief history of the Kingdom of Saudi Arabia that age-old call of both lamentation and exaltation was heard throughout the land when the death of H.M. King Sa'ud ibn Abd al-'Aziz ibn Muhammad came about in November of 1953 in Tayif. Immediately his son, Crown Prince Sa'ud Ibn Abd Al Aziz, was pronounced King of Arabia, a decision the founder had made 20 years earlier in 1933. Thus the peaceful dynastic succession of the House of Saud began, much as the doughty old warrior-king had conceived it. The country remained calm.

In early 1954, it was rumored that King Sa'ud would visit Al Hasa Province as part of a tour of the principal parts of his kingdom, especially Hofuf, the seat of the governor of that eastern province, Shaikh 'Abd Allah ibn Jiluwi (his father's cousin who had helped him capture Riyadh late in 1902). The king was expected to visit Aramco's oil operations, the bulk of which were also in Al Hasa, near Dhahran.

Things were beginning to happen in Dhahran.

A triumphal archway of

Members of the Royal Family stroll beside Budd Cars as SAGRR officials review procedures for the day.

steel, wood, and fabric was taking shape at warp speed adjacent to Dhahran's main gate, spanning both lines of traffic. It wasn't the Arc De Triumph, the Diocletian Gates, or the Hanging Gardens of Babylon, but when completed, it would be massive, of good proportions and design, and clad in the traditional colors of Saudi Arabia—green and white. A message of welcome from the Arabian American Oil Company (Aramco) was to top off the impressive structure, surmounted by several Saudi national flags. There wasn't much time for anything more, that was clear.

This feverish activity (and lots more being organized in other quarters, it was rumored) was to honor the impending visit of King Sa'ud, his first visit to Dhahran since his succession to the throne. I learned that I was to be directly involved in at least one event.

On Sunday morning, January 3, when I arrived at the office, Tommy F. Walters was already there, waiting for me. He was the chief photographer for the public relations department; I was his backup, sharing assignments with him as they came in the door.

"There's a nice, easy, simple assignment coming up real soon that I think you can handle without

even having to think about it," he said.

"O.K," I said. "I'll buy that. How soon, and what is it?"

"It's tomorrow," he said. "The King will be leaving Riyadh on his way down here, stopping off in Hofuf to visit Shaikh Ibn Jiluwi for a few days. Then he'll be coming from there to visit us in Dhahran."

Tom explained that I'd have to go to Riyadh that afternoon, taking the Budd car from Dammam. Once in Riyadh, I was to check into Baker Camp at the airport, spend the night there and board the same Budd car the following morning long before the king and his entourage showed up.

My assignment was to secure—somehow—the first new portrait of the king since he succeeded to the throne. Just where this request had originated was in doubt but a new, current picture would have many uses both for the Saudi government and Aramco, once secured. I just hoped all the necessary clearances were in place so that my showing up wouldn't be took much of a surprise. As almost an afterthought, Tom suggested that I should try to shoot pictures of other members of the royal family, those who might be new counselors to the king, currently unknown to Aramco. Be discreet, he urged.

I went home, packed a green Aramco bag with a change of clothing, shaving gear, and a toothbrush, and loaded up my camera bag with plenty of film, new batteries, and extra flashbulbs. About mid-afternoon Tom drove me to Dammam, where I climbed onto the sleek new silver, self-propelled Budd, the latest passenger cars of the Saudi Arabian Government Railroad (SAGRR).

"Take it easy, now," he said. "It'll happen, you'll get the shot."

"What if I don't?"

"Well, just don't bother to come back!"

The trip up—about five hours—was pleasant and uneventful, the Budd car gliding over the new single track, almost silent except for the hum of the electric motors and whisper of the air-conditioning in each car. The large picture windows offered an impressive view of the desert, virtually uninhabited except for a few black tents of the Bedouin and occasionally small trains of camels traversing the flat almost featureless desert, not a single, tiny oasis of palm trees that might signify water. The afternoon sun, at its most blistering, beat down on everything as the Budd car (its own cool, self-contained, movable oasis) sped westward toward Riyadh,. Later that evening I checked into Baker Camp, the transient facilities at the airport, had dinner and set my alarm for six a.m.

I boarded the Budd car about 7 a.m., the morning quite cool and pleasant, about average for January. I walked through the three connected Budd cars. One served as a dining room, a long table running down the middle of the car, with china, silver, and napkins bearing the royal crest already in place, enough to seat about 20 people. Another car had open seating with comfortable window seats and more big windows. The third car appeared to have several private compartments, no doubt for the king, his counselors, and guests. I noticed a good-sized kitchen/galley at the rear.

Things were taking place outside. A small truck drove up and what looked like foodstuffs were being unloaded. A detachment of soldiers began to assemble, their rifles with fixed bayonets in place. Two of the King's bodyguards had arrived, both wearing full length

Kind Sa'ud arrives at Hofuf, where he is greeted by an honor guard, which he acknowledges with a salute.

brocaded outer garments, their chests criss-crossed with bullet-laden bandoleers. Each wore a dagger at the waist and carried a sword in one hand, in the other a machine pistol of some type. They sat on the steps of one of the Budd cars, large, powerful, and silent men, waiting. Another two men stood nearby, holding small braziers in their hands, smoke curling up from the incense being burnt. I caught a glimpse of John H. Gildea, manager of the SAGRR, walking alongside the track, accompanied by his tall Palestinian interpreter, and another assistant.

Suddenly from out of nowhere, several black Cadillacs swept into the station, stopping close to the Budd cars. Doors opened and bodyguards tumbled out, about eight, all surrounding one of the cars. The rear door of this car opened, the king struggled out, turned briefly to acknowledge the honor guard presenting arms, and climbed aboard the train. Members of his entourage quickly boarded at other points. Within minutes the station was clear of people. Two minutes later we were under way. I picked one of the rear seats in the public car next to a window, watched and waited.

I had yet to see Shaikh Abdullah Bulkhair, the man who was going to make this trip worthwhile for me. The king's personal secretary,

a title that might not sound too important, he was the person who made access to Ibn Sa'ud a very real possibility. Not a large man, Shaikh Abdullah was powerful, trusted by the king, influential, and accessible. He spoke English well, had traveled extensively, and was a force to be aware of at all times.

I began to stroll about a bit (without cameras), taking a head count to see how many people were aboard and to see how many I did know. There were about 35 people, but I identified very few. As I continued wending my way toward what I assumed to be the king's compartment, Abdullah Bulkhair appeared, greeted me and, knowing my assignment without my having to remind him, said one word, "Later." I indicated I wanted to take some general pictures, which he agreed to and then waved me on my way. I returned to get my cameras.

Everything went well. I nodded to people, most of whom were seated, and indicated that I wanted to photograph them. They nodded in approval and arranged themselves accordingly, with no exchange of words required. Some smiled, most tried to look at ease, only one or two looked disagreeable. I came upon five bodyguards together in the dining car and photographed them both seated and, at my request, standing. It would make for a powerful picture, I thought. These were men who I had seen at Naziriyah Palace, com-

Bodyguards gather around the dining table, waiting for His Majesty to appear.

pleted last year for the then-crown prince. As I moved back toward the private compartments, I came upon Prince Mishaal, the minister of defense, who readily agreed to be photographed.

A t another point in my travels, I almost bumped into a handsome young fellow, obviously a member of the royal family, who was about to enter one of the private units. I tapped my camera, but he smiled, shook his head, then nevertheless invited me into the compartment. He sat down and spoke to me in English.

He said something along the lines that it would be inappropriate for him to be photographed, which I thought might be because of religious scruples. I replied that that was fine, but also remarked that his English was excellent.

"Yes," he said, "I learned my English listening to Teresa Brewer songs."

Budd car operator prepares to leave Riyadh, Royal party on board.

At which point he broke into song, singing a couple of stanzas from her most recent popular song, with the following lyrics. "Come onna my house, I wanna make you happy!" I laughed out loud, as he did. I asked him his name, but he refused to divulge it. He then told me that he had learned English while detained at King Abdul Aziz's pleasure in Riyadh, but had been released under a general amnesty declared by the new king. (Later on, when luncheon was served I did not see him at the table.) He did not reveal the reason for his detention. I went on my way, waiting for the call from Shaikh Abdullah.

It came shortly after lunch, where the king sat at the head of the table and stayed chatting with various guests and staff members for some time. (Usually the king at the palace was served first, finished first, and then immediately left the table, which signified the end of the meal. Sometimes some people never got dessert.)

Following the king's return to his quarters, Shaikh Abdullah beckoning me to join him. I pushed my way through bodyguards, guests, and others standing in the narrow corridor. I was advised that I had just a few minutes to get my picture. With that warning I entered the small suite and sized up the situation. The king nodded

Luncheon is served aboard the Budd car on way to Hofuf.

Waiter keep an eye on honor guard awaiting arrival of king.

One of King Sa'ud's personal bodyguards relaxes for a moment, as the air-conditioned Budd car speeds across the desert.

The governor of Al Hasa Province, Shaikh Abdullah Ibn Jiluwi, host of the king's first visit to the principle oil-producing area since his ascension to the throne, traveled with the monarch from Riyadh—a pleasant trip of several hours.

to me, offering a small smile.

He was wearing the traditional brown woolen bisht, edged in gold, and a gutra and egal, and was seated in front of a large window. Behind him was another, smaller window, partially closed by drapes, which looked awkward and untidy. I quickly moved behind him, brought the drapes together as best as possible to provide a uniform backdrop. Once more in front, I framed him in the Rollei, filled most of the square format with his head, shoulders, and upper chest, and prepared to shoot, using single flashbulbs bounced off the ceiling for an even, shadowless picture. He looked awfully grim, I thought.

Following the first exposure and as I replaced the spent flashbulb, I said. "One more please."

Suddenly the king turned to Bulkhair and said, "Aysh Haada, 'one more?'" (What does that mean?)

Bulkhair leaned into the King and said, "Ba'ad Wahid, min fadlik."

With that King Sa'ud smiled, repeated the phrase, chuckled out loud and relaxed a bit more, finally offering me a pleasant smile. I popped the second bulb.

The next shot I said, "Ba'ad Wahid, Minfadlick."

At this point, Shaikh Abdullah signaled that the session was over. Barely five minutes. It was a close call.

An hour or so later, as the Budd cars pulled into Hofuf, the king was greeted by a military honor guard complete with band, all led by Ibn Jiluwi, his host for the next few days.

I continued on to Dhahran, rushed to the photo lab to process the film and found to my great relief that the last frame was the best of the three. I printed it, along with a selection of others taken during the trip, just meeting the deadline of the Arabian Sun and Flare, which was about to go to press. The lead article of the weekly welcomed the king's arrival in Dhahran, featured the portrait and reported that the new monarch and his entourage would remain in the area for about two weeks before departing by car on a hunting trip in the north, then back to Riyadh.

Mothers, school teachers, and a soldier provide all types of crowd control as the frisky youngsters await the arrival of the king and his party at Steineke Hall, Dhahran.

The new portrait was put to good use in many conventional ways. One of the most surprising was discovering it on the face of a watch several months later, when I (and other members of a motion picture crew) received one, along with a handsome bisht, gutra, and egal, and several gold sovereigns following a ten-day stint in Riyadh shooting footage of the king for the movie Island of Oil. And on at least two subsequent occasions when I photographed the king, he saw me approaching and called out with considerable glee, "Ya, Ba'ad Wahid!"

The large tower was a reminder of the elaborate radio-telephone system installed by the late King Ibn Sa'ud, which kept him in constant touch with key points of his kingdom. Troops and bodyguards stand by at Damman.

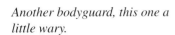

Another bodyguard, this one a little wary.

Prince Mishaal, in his compartment.

King Sa'ud visited Dhahran for several days as a guest of Aramco. Here he was entertained by American students singing songs, who were followed by Saudi students reciting poems. A small son of the king, ignoring the protocols of the day, spontaneously sneaked in to give his father a kiss.

The new portrait.

Tapline

A freelance writer—Phil Gustafson, from New York City—had been invited to visit Badanah in Northwestern Saudi Arabia to view the spring arrival of hundreds of Bedouins, their families, and thousands of camels and other livestock who planned to feast on the new, succulent vegetation that for a few short days turned the desert green. It was thought to be soon, perhaps imminent, but the Americans did not know exactly when. Only the Bedouin seemed to know. Although even they had some doubts. When asked, they had an answer.

"Bukra, inshalla." (Tomorrow, if God is willing.)

The arrival of the camels and the full, timely blossoming of the desert was a carefully calculated, precious happening. It was as though the Bedouin tribes and nature itself had to be in harmony if the maximum benefit was to be derived from this annual event. Timing was all-important, the visit eagerly awaited, a powerful reminder of the life cycles of the nomadic tribesmen, who counted so much on the rare generosity of the harsh desert.

Overnight, a small vanguard of the nomads had arrived. The early morning light revealed several long black tents already erected, others being assembled, dotting the flat featureless desert some distance from the village. New sounds filled the air, that of children playing near their tents, and the raucous grumbling of camels as they came awake. Later that day, we climbed the silver water tower at the pump station so that the arrival of the visitors could be observed. Only a few were seen straggling in, little else on the horizon. Bukra?

A handsome Bedouin youth, one of the first to arrive at Badanah in search of forage.

Badanah was one of four pumping stations built by Trans Arabian Pipeline which was begun in 1948 and completed in 1950. The other three—Qaisumah, Rafah, and Turaif—were separated by about 200 miles of desert, close to the Neutral Zone, Iraq, Jordan, and Syria, finally crossing Lebanon. Their function was simple: to push a half-million barrels of oil daily through a 30–31 inch pipeline beginning in Ras Tanura and ending its 1,067 mile journey on the shores of Sidon, Lebanon. Here a giant tank farm sat on a hill as oil tankers lined the horizon of the azure blue of the Mediterranean Sea, waiting their turn to take on oil for destinations throughout much of Europe.

Gustafson's visit would enable him to spend a couple of days with the few Americans who operated this remote pumping station, who lived with their wives and children in their own air-conditioned homes just a short distance from the nearby Arab village. There was virtually no social contact between the villagers and the Americans although the superintendent of the station made frequent courtesy calls upon the emir, in charge of the Northern Frontier, based in 'Ar'ar. He lived in a somewhat more substantial home befitting his stature, along with his family, retainers, and soldiers, barely a couple of miles away. The two communities lived separate, self-contained lives, respecting each other's privacy. The writer would visit both as he waited for the desert to bloom.

There were about a dozen Americans, most with wives, at this outpost. They were engineers, plant operators, and technicians who monitored the pumps that controlled the continuous flow of product. Another 25 employees, principally Saudis, were receiving on-the-job training that would enable them to replace the Americans. The pipeline was the largest crude oil pipeline ever built in the world, eliminating the need for tankers to travel more than 3,000 miles via the Suez Canal, a round trip of eighteen days. Some major economies there, it was clear.

Life for the Americans and their families was remote, restricted, and limited. It called for a great deal of self-reliance in order to prevail over the loneliness of the assignment. There was a commissary, a mess-hall, a baseball diamond, and golf courses at a couple of the locations. Schools for the children were established. Movies were shown. The weekly milkrun of DC-3s hedgehopping to every Tapline pump station brought supplies, mail, and anything else required. It was easy to hitch a free ride into Beirut for a few days vacation, which made life much more bearable. If you couldn't cope, you moved on with no hard feelings or recriminations. Many people stayed on and did their jobs, saved a nice nest egg and retired.

If there were interruptions to the physical flow of oil, most of them could be solved by engineers on site or specialists brought in from Beirut or Dhahran. If the problems were political in nature, they were addressed by the government relations departments of Tapline or Aramco, in concert with the emir. Mr. Gustafson spent the next day visiting the village, which had come into existence largely as a result of establishing the pumping station. He met the emir, who was about to set off on a hunting trip, accompanied by a few soldiers and a handler with two of the emir's favorite falcons. He observed the local butcher dressing a sheep he had just slaughtered, in anticipation of the arrival of the visitors. By nightfall, a few more Bedouin had arrived.

A scattering of new tents could be seen the following morning, the desert itself still barren of new growth, some camels freely grazing while a few more assembled at one of the older wells. A visit was made to the local office of Aramco's government relations department, where a guest from Dhahran was reviewing matters with the emir's representative. Neither yielded little news.

We offered, "Bukra?" They came back with, "Inshalla!"

On the third day, still nothing, with the milkrun due the following day on its regular run. Mr. Gustafson revealed that he had pressing business in Manhattan, so it was decided that if the desert had not bloomed by morning, he would depart for Dhahran and then on to New York. If it did, he would stay. On day four, there were no signs of the greening of the desert. We boarded the DC-3 and headed back to Dhahran.

Two days later, Badanah advised that the desert had finally burst into bloom with the Bedouin arriving in great numbers, right on time to take full advantage of nature's bounty. We informed Phil Gustafson of this glorious happening, who responded with the little Arabic he had picked up during his abortive visit.

"Allah, Akbar!" (God is Great!)

Welcome to Badanah. (Every station has a similar sign that extols safety)

No one can deny the joys of a simple swing, especially with Mom.

The emir is the princip and meets frequently w

How's this for a pretty special schoolhouse, reminiscent of similar little centers of learning that dotted the American prairies years ago?

Homes sit between the plant and the open desert, where the black tents of visiting Bedouin are their occasional visitors during the year.

56

The village of Badanah.

The emir's representative welcomes Tapline staff members to his office with a glass of tea.

This man had come to see thousands of camels feast on the rare gifts of the desert.

...thority in the area, which shares for many miles a common border with Iraq. He lives close to the station and the village ...pline managers and staff. An avid hunter, he is very proud of his falcons.

This young lad gives off a confident smile, while his sister is a little less assured.

Within sight of the station, visitors congregate at a wadi to carry out a variety of chores.

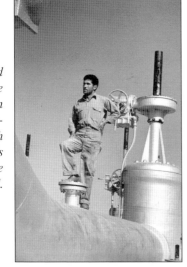

Operating and maintaining the pumping station was a 24-hour-a-day job which called for skills that, over time, the Saudi mastered.

The pipeline required constant surveillance to ensure the continuous flow of crude oil.

A new lifestyle that offered wages, a home, better health, and a longer life, took time to absorb.

The pumping station, painted a silvery-aluminum that glistens day and night, is the most prominent feature within a thousand square miles of nothing.

William R. Chandler, president.

Oscar Swanson, chief accountant.

Dr. Frank Zukowski, medical director.

Frank Bates, senior counsel.

Capt. J.R. Jones, supt. Sidon Terminal.

Col. William Eddy, political consultant.

Come morning, the numbers are low and the desert shows little sign of greening.

As the sun goes down, a few more Bedouin straggle in with their camels in close order behind.

Small boys run for the sheer joy of it or for fear of a Jinn.

Life for the Bedouin, perhaps especially for the young, is harsh, but a momentary grin in the midst of hardship can be infectious.

This new camel trough, ready and waiting attracted only a few villagers waiting for the desert to bloom.

In the early light, the first Bedouin tents attract a few villagers, mostly children.

Romance

Following the ceremony, everyone is clearly in a joyful mood, especially the bride and groom.

Infrastructure meant many things.

Almost from the very beginning of the arrival of women employees, a strange phenomenon occurred at Dhahran Airport. A number of bachelors, somehow learning that another batch of females was due in on the company plane (which came in twice weekly, either the Gazelle or Camel), began to show up at the airport to observe. Few of these men had any real business at the airport, but a good number had trucks and could conveniently stop by the airport at just at the right time. Most of them looked unusually neat, were wearing clean khakis or whites, and had obviously shaved that morning. A self-appointed welcoming committee, you might say.

Aramco faced many challenges in those early days Among the thousand and one separate tasks it had to tackle—exclusive of searching for oil—included the following: It had to—over time—build homes, commissaries, post offices, schools, public libraries, barber (and beauty) shops, laundry and dry cleaning facilities and for a while, at least, maintain a beverage store. It built theatres, swimming pools, eventually an 18-hole golf course, baseball diamonds, football fields, and other recreational facilities.

And then, once built, it had the responsibility of managing or governing what became three permanent communities, providing the services demanded by its population, much like any other small village, town, or municipality in the United States. Services included light, power, garbage collection, sewage, air conditioning—and even security.

At the same time, or prior to or concurrent with, Aramco needed to people these communities with lots of Americans. Construction stiffs, office managers, geologists, roustabouts, engineers, draftsmen, mechanics, lathe

operators, pilots, cooks, plumbers, accountants, all jobs were at that time filled by males. Hundreds of job classifications, thousands of men. And then there were the assignments traditionally filled by women: secretaries, nurses, keypunch operators, school teachers, payroll clerks, and numerous other office-related tasks.

Fortunately, the Saudi government had agreed to allow American women (and, later, other nationalities) to enter the country and work for Aramco, though some restrictions were applied to them. Thus was created for the first time ever, a microcosm of a homogeneous society typical of America. They were Christian and, by all accounts, conservative in politics and morality, reflective of that fifties era. If the Ulema or clerics fretted about the role or behavior of women employees, they could look with confidence at the conduct of the very first American women who joined their husbands during the latter days of exploring Arabia for oil.

These few women, most of them all too familiar with the hardships of isolation and separation that their husbands' professions imposed, signaled in yet another way to the Saudi government that the Americans were going to stay.

But the women soon discovered that the task of planting roots, creating a new home, and introducing some semblance of American life in Arabia would require almost superhuman efforts for them to prevail over its unique,

(left) Romance begat matrimony, which (if blessed), brought forth progeny, followed by community, stability and, inevitably, school buses.

Betrothed off to Bahrain, courtesy of Aramco Convair (cost, $15 each).

T. F. Walters

Martha Holderman makes bridegroom presentable.

T. F. Walters

Everybody looked petrified, so best man (Michael Cheney) thought it best to close his eyes.

T. F. Walters

T. F. Walters

hostile environment. Most succeeded.

As for the notion that large numbers of single women would eventually be recruited by Aramco to work in Arabia, that was a bit more difficult to imagine. The logical and inescapable fact that romance would flourish as a result was not argued. The offspring of such unions was another inevitability. That being born in Arabia might provide them the option of dual nationality—Saudi Arabian and American—was intriguing.

It all came to pass when the first planeload of single women deplaned at Dhahran Airport. There were 26 of them, from all parts of America. All had signed up to serve a minimum of two years in the field, agreeing to be sent anywhere within the country as required by the needs of Aramco. Most stayed in Dhahran, some went to Ras Tanura, a few to Abqaiq. Not all of them were young, nor was everyone a raving beauty, but all of them had been evaluated by recruiters as being able to withstand the unique demands that would be placed on them in a hostile natural environment, in a culture that would largely be beyond their reach. Some might find a loneliness that just might tip the scale too far in the wrong direction. Perhaps the members of the welcoming committee put some at ease.

For them, it was impossible to effect any sort of introduction to any one of them as they were carefully shepherded through Saudi customs. Just the simple pleasure of seeing a number of attractive, single girls arriving, gave one hope at the possibility of meeting some of them. No one knew to which district these females might be assigned. Some say it inspired these bachelors to put up with

the heat and other frustrations of daily life. Hey, life in Arabia might have some meaning after all, these stoics reasoned.

Aramco's management might have been thinking somewhat along the same lines. But there wasn't a chance in Hades to think that the structure and pattern of life in Arabia might approximate in any way the imperially rarefied atmosphere of the British Raj, or the highly suspect social order prevailing in the Anglo-Iranian Oil Company in Iran. Aramco was going to do it the American way, to ensure the creation of a highly stable work force of professional men and women essential to carrying out the numerous and diverse and complex requirements of a brand-new oil industry.

It wasn't long before an embryonic social life sprang up, generated by the typical drive and character of Americans to create organizations and clubs and special interest activities to achieve the stated objectives of the organization (aided and abetted every step of the way by Aramco). The basic idea was to extract as much joy, pleasure, and satisfaction from a given activity, whether it was new or different, tough or easy. Usually competitive, sometimes not, the best ideals of America were coming into play.

Sports was big: golf, tennis, fencing, baseball, soccer, sailing, scuba diving, fishing, the list seemed endless. And philately, photography, painting, sculpture, music, amateur theatricals. Swimming, competitive or casual. Reading was a given, movies a must, carefully selected though they might have been. Good conversation of

all types in great abundance at every type of meeting or gathering. A microcosm of America was in the making, sophisticated and so-so.

And then there was romance, best exemplified publicly by dancing on the patio, with music provided by records, most of it almost current with America. All that was missing at such public manifestations were cocktails, the lack of them about the only reminder that liquor was not permitted at such open events. The music was—at that point in time—definitely American. Dancing itself was a natural, albeit somewhat discrete activity, again a reflection of the era—early fifties from one perspective. Cutting in was permitted in good spirits. Disagreements were exceedingly rare; brawls nonexistent. Self discipline and good behavior of everyone was exemplary. Civility was securely in place.

The practice of dating was carried out in public, through all the venues noted. Affairs were another thing, usually carried out with great discretion, with some shock value when they became public. Overt behavior other than wholly heterosexual, was not suffered and led to prompt departure from the field. For those who spent time calculating the odds, marriage was almost an inevitable consequence.

In time, engagements were announced, parties given, information about the time and place of the nuptials was divulged. In view of the fact that Christian worship (which included marriage) could not be conducted in Arabia, the options for elsewhere in the world were plentiful. The idea of getting married in India, or Ceylon, or Beirut, Lebanon, intrigued the engaged couple. So why not Swit-

Moment of truth.

It's true! Women are more beautiful when they are pregnant.

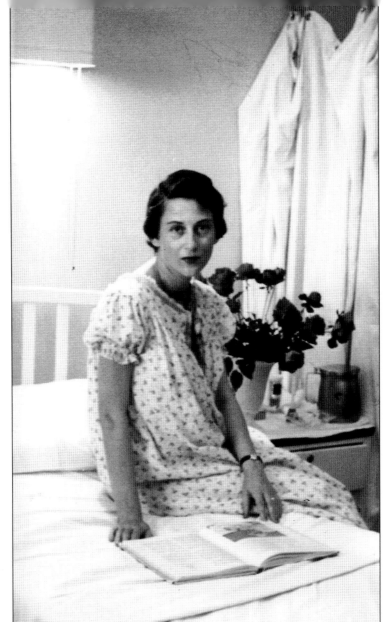

Delivered.

Cassandra Lea.

zerland, or France, even England. Sometimes families at home influenced the choice. Quite often, the event was planned to coincide with the long leave earned by one or both of the betrothed.

Somehow, housing became available, perhaps temporary (house sitting for long vacationers) and then permanent.

Thus, another element of American civilization, a crucial part of natural society—an all important fragment of the total infrastructure that was the responsibility of Aramco—took root and flourished.

No need for a dryer in these climes.

Paris

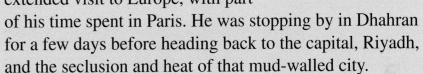

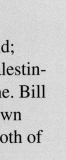

The Eiffel Tower.

The first vacation earned by new Aramcoms was often a life-saver, as the two-week holiday—usually spent in France, England, or Spain—made the return to Arabia for another year quite bearable. At least one person in Riyadh felt the same way.

It was Paris, on a day that was gray and cloudy. It had been raining and the dark surface of the road glistened. A black Cadillac stood at the curb outside the George V hotel. A small Saudi Arabian flag hung damply from the front stanchion of the glistening limousine.

The scene panned to the entrance of the hotel and zoomed in close as the glass door swung open wide. A figure, draped in the conventional suiting worn by all Saudis, walked smartly onto the pavement, looked directly at us, smiled a dazzling smile, waved grandly, turned to duck into the limousine. The waiting chauffeur closed the door soundlessly and climbed into the front seat. The car, slowly accelerating, moved away from us in complete silence and disappeared from view.

Another shift of view and we were at the base of the

Prince Talal bin Abdul Aziz (half brother to King Fahd).

Eiffel Tower. We crawled up one side of it with our lens and back down, cutting to another close-up of the featured player: Prince Talal bin Abdul Aziz, younger brother of King Sa'ud. Talal's face completely filled the frame, a young man about 30 years old with a pencil-thin mustache, wearing glasses with thick lenses. He smiled broadly and beckoned us to accompany him. We were captives anyway, so we went along.

We entered a waiting elevator, and with the prince holding a large cigar in one hand, we slowly climbed upward. We surveyed in turn the Palace de Chaillot, the Seine, and in the distance, Montmartre, with the church of the Sacre Couer gleaming whitely. This was my first visit to Paris in two years and my first ever on the Eiffel Tower. It was grand. I settled back in my seat.

When the elevator stopped and the door opened, the prince ran toward the parapet and made as if to throw himself over the side. The camera followed the action, changing to another close-up, continuing over the edge and sweeping down to the plaza below. Then back to the terrace, where the prince, laughing exuberantly, was being urged way from the edge, presumably by a staff member of the Saudi embassy.

The silence of the moment was broken with the clatter of film and the whir of an empty spool, which brought us

back to reality. The lights clicked on and I looked back at the film projector where Prince Talal was busily changing reels. It appears that he had just returned from an extended visit to Europe, with part of his time spent in Paris. He was stopping by in Dhahran for a few days before heading back to the capital, Riyadh, and the seclusion and heat of that mud-walled city.

A guest of Aramco, he was staying at one of the several houses maintained by the oil company. Air-conditioned, completely furnished, the pleasant ranch-type dwellings were temporary homes to frequent visitors from many lands. We were seated in the dining area, with the furniture moved back to provide space for the portable screen at one end of the room. At the other end was a table with the 16mm film projector sitting on it. All the window blinds were drawn.

There were seven of us: Prince Talal; Bill McDonald; Aramco's government relations representative; a Palestinian interpreter; three of the prince's servants; and me. Bill and I were offered a drink but getting a warning frown from McDonald, I refused. If it had been alcohol, both of us would have been in an embarrassing position.

As we talked with the prince, we agreed with him that the film (black and white) was excellent and asked who had shot them. Talal informed us that he had hired a French television cameraman to document his visit to Paris. An enthusiastic amateur still photographer, he had decided to use the medium of motion pictures (rather than still pictures) to document forever the wonderful trip. We nodded sympathetically, knowing full well the restorative value of a local leave.

As the next roll was threaded and ready to run, we hunched down in our seats, smiled appreciatively as the prince turned off the lights and hit the projector switch. The screen splashed with full color, a surprise.

Yes, this was in color, and here was the prince, apparently in his suite at the George V, seated at breakfast wearing a tiger striped dressing gown and a bright red golfing cap. Now reading a newspaper. Now smiling at us. We laughed and smiled right back at him. The room exploded with laughter.

We cut to the Tuileries and found him walking ahead of us, arms around two young girls—a blonde and a redhead. He began to skip, then danced along, stopped, kissed one extravagantly, and then turned to face the camera. A close up revealed that the girls were extremely pretty and, surprisingly, rather shy.

But after a moment they began to make faces at the camera and to smile and chatter sound-

A local leave in Paris during the fifties was an exhilarating experience that met every expectation. Its unique ambience immediately restored one's faith in the meaning of life. All that followed—superb food, great wines, marvelous architecture, the simple joy of strolling the streets, peering into shop windows—was a tonic. For many, coffee and a croissant at a sidewalk cafe would be a memory that would not wither but sustain one for a long time, if not forever.

lessly to us. The girls waved as if to say goodbye and passed out of the scene. Another cut, this time to an interior of a nightclub with a Middle Eastern motif, the camera panning slowly around the interior, pausing at a group shot of some 12 to 15 girls. There, right in the middle of them, dressed this time in a neat blue suit, with a striped tie, was our host. Looking just like any other Middle Eastern businessman on holiday in Paris. He was smiling.

We covered more of Paris on foot, jumped on and off trolleys, hailed cabs and dispensed with them. We stopped many times, looked up, down, and around, all through our single eye. We enjoyed his vacation, or at least some part of it.

When this second roll was finished, I decided to leave. Thanking him for the entertainment, I promised to return in two days with the pictures taken of him earlier that afternoon. Bring only those in which he is smiling, he insisted. Bill remained, as he was still on duty.

Outside the house, I offered the interpreter a ride home. We drove down King's Row and headed for Intermediate Camp. Turning a corner onto his street, something rolled out from under the front seat. It was a bottle. As I put the brake on, another one came rolling out and clanked against the first. I picked both of them up and

While taxis were the preferred mode of transportation, a bus bowling along a boulevard in Paris reminded one of the life and vitality of the City of Light.

placed them on the seat between us.

At his quarters, I stopped and let him out. He looked at me without saying a word. Was he a Muslim or a Christian, I wondered. I handed him one of the bottles, said good night and drove home. With the lemons that had just come in at the commissary, it would be nice to have a sour before dinner.

By a strange coincidence, some 43 years later, Prince Talal's son, Prince Alwaled bin Talal Abdul Aziz al Saud, bought the George V for $167 million and spent another $125 million on refurbishing this "mythic Paris hotel." It is run by Four Seasons Hotels and Resorts, as reported in Vanity Fair.

The pictures used to illustrate this piece (excluding the portrait of Prince Talal), were taken in Paris during a similar local leave enjoyed by the author and his wife.

The artist carries on, aware only of his subject (unless someone wants to buy, perhaps).

Bookstalls along the Seine demand that you find something for your bookshelf back in Dhahran or Ras Tanura.

If you don't like magnificent architecture, you don't belong in Paris.

The Church of the Sacre Coeur. Climbing these steps is rewarding for young and old, as the view of Paris from the very top is inspirational.

Portraits: Royal Family

Someone said that the new palace being built in Riyadh for the crown prince was nearing completion. Somebody else thought it might be a good idea to take some photographs of it and offer them as a goodwill gesture. Another person averred that movies might be even better. In due time, it came about that both a still photographer and a motion picture cameraman were advised to plan for an exploratory visit to Naziriyah, on the outskirts of the capital city.

The idea had been well received in Riyadh, with minor reservations. It was important that some ground rules be established to determine just how this film team should proceed. The palace was already in daily use, thus some care was required in determining just what would be available to be photographed, how, and at what times during the day or evening.

Shaikh Abdullah Bulkhair, the crown prince's private secretary, conducted a tour of portions of the palace. The dining room was very large, at which everyone was entitled to eat (including photographers); the number of rooms, suites, and meeting places, too many to count. Most decorated in large, baroque period furniture. Ac-

Naziriyah, the crown prince's new palace, Riyadh (March '52).

cess to a portion of the women's quarters—beautiful, all white, several stories high and wonderfully cool—was limited. Empty except for one lone woman seated on the floor, sewing in a corner of a courtyard open to the sky, this portion of the palace would not be available.

The grounds were still being planted with a variety of flowers, soon to be finished. It might be possible to see some of the crown prince's horses, some of which were brought through the gardens in the evening, it was noted. A swimming pool appeared to be finished but was empty of water. An attractive cabana overlooked it but seemed a bit incongruous for the overall setting. It was suggested that as the crown prince was very proud of the activities at Al Kharj, it would be valuable to spend some time there.

Lunch with the crown prince (and many others) was very pleasant, although always seated well below the salt. Meals were served Western style, with cutlery for all. Dessert, often ice cream, was a gamble. The crown prince at the head table was served first and, when finished, rarely spent time conversing with his guests or counselors. Once he rose to leave, everyone else did.

The three-week visit went well.

(left) King Sa'ud, in the center of the photograph, surrounded by members of the royal family and the public, has just inspected the first four Convair aircraft of the newly created Saudi Arabian Airline.

69

The façade of Naziriyah, with cameraman setting up shot.

Prince Addullah in garden.

One of ever-present bodyguards.

Young prince (left) and playmate.

Portrait of even younger prince.

King Sa'ud flanked by palace officials, counselors, officers, and bodyguards.

Shaikh Abdullah Suleiman, legendary finance minister who signed original concession agreement.

Shaikh Abdulla Ibn Adwan, deputy minister of finance and national economy.

Several counselors, including Shaikh Addullah Bulkhair, bottom right (king's personal secretary).

Members of royal family arrive by Cadillac at Dammam.

The king arrives, welcomed by Shaikh Abdullah Ib'n Jiluwi, governor of Al Hasa Province (helping young princes from car).

The royal entourage and guests view a camel race.

Fred A. Davies, right, and His Majesty, enjoy a glass of hot tea.

Troops, officers, bodyguards, servants, and townspeople await arrival of Sa'ud.

The king, at the head of the banquet table.

His Majesty notes that Floyd Ohliger and Fred Davies have found a little gristle, one of the perils of protocol.

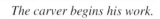

The carver begins his work.

Tables for that evening are decorated with fruit.

Village and cultivated acreage seen from Al Kharj Farm, much expanded over the years.

Produce ready to be delivered to the palace and other royal households.

Introduction of Santa Gertrudas improved quality and yield of cattle.

The magical incubator.

Home on the range.

Future farmers of Al Kharj finish their studies for the day.

More water, more produce.

A farm pet, not for the table!

Mother, with new-born calf.

Pheasants in abundance.

…and more of them.

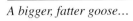
A bigger, fatter goose…

75

Listening for Oil

A geologist's life in the fifties in Saudi Arabia was a far cry from the challenges faced by such pioneers as Max Steineke, Krug Henry, Tom Barger, and several others. But it was still a testing experience that demanded the best a guy had in him.

For many of the newer, younger members of the exploration department, that search for new (or age-old, to be more precise) deposits of oil seemed for a number of years to be continuous and they were never-ending all under the management of O.A. "Cottie" Seager.

At any one time, there might be from four to six self-contained exploratory units out in the desert, spending up to six weeks at a time at different points, one week back in town. Then out again for another six. The units might include surface parties (G-1), seismic parties (S-1), gravity-meter/magnetometer parties (GM-1) and structural drill parties.

The size of these units could vary from two geologists, a few Saudis, and a small detachment of soldiers, to perhaps ten Americans, 50 or 60 Saudis, and a similarly small body of soldiers, depending on the function of the team. Bill Brown, who spent about four years with various units in new and different parts of the desert, remembers it as being "hotter than blazes [125 degrees in the

shade]…when we sat up all night shooting the stars for position location.," pretty much the same that Tom Barger was doing in the early thirties (as he reported in his letters to his wife, Kathleen).

A structure drill unit (#4) assembles outside Dhahran for a final check before heading off into the desert.

During certain periods of the year, there would be heard the incessant drone of a lone, multiengined aircraft flying back and forth across the sky in certain sectors of the kingdom, mapping for the first time ever through aerial photography those portions of the country approved in the original concession agreement. This work was carried out for Aramco under contract by the U.S. Geological Service, the exposed film developed daily, from which large (8" x 8") black-and-white prints were made by automatic printers.

Eventually the desert yielded up its subterranean secrets to these men traversing the sand dunes and gravel plains as they carried out their assignments, beginning at about

7 a.m. every day. One of the first and most important functions was the early morning radio call into Dhahran to report on progress, problems, and plans for that day. Some of the units were visited regularly by a milk-run DC-3, which could usually find a firm gravel strip close enough and long enough to handle the landing and take-off of the plane. (Not all units got this treatment.) An average work-day was about eight–ten hours long, although the structure drill parties apparently went at it 24 hours a day.

The food was good and the air-conditioned trailer(s) a godsend. The crews came across animals: rabbits, gazelles, lizards, snakes, qata (see page 106), but very few ever saw the now-fabled oryx, which had been hunted out in the last couple of decades (a few exist in captivity). Some pistols and shotguns were carried, often at the discretion of the crew boss, though there were more musical instruments brought along by crew members. Fresh-killed gazelle was a nice change of menu, many agreed.

But everybody pretty much agreed that desert life was far better than sitting around in an air-conditioned office in Dhahran. And the Bedouin profited from the stratigraphic tests conducted, as many brought forth water. Completed as wells for the nomads, they were mightily impressed.

As the campsite is established, a Bedouin stopped by to visit. The cook invited him to sell them a young camel, which the Bedouin agrees to deliver in a few days.

Off to the showers.

A gazelle, shot on the way to the campsite, pleases the cook.

Visitors relax outside their tent at end of the day.

Getting stuck in soft sand is typical, requires much patience, some serious traction—and help.

One of the first elements erected is the portable drilling rig, which often operates 24 hours a day.

Racks of pipe are carried on the sides of the rig.

A new drilling bit is installed.

A Saudi operator hustles up and down the rig installing pipe as required.

Selecting, collecting, assembling pipe is a ballet all its own.

Cables with sensors attached are laid out on the desert according to plan.

Screwing together a number of explosive canisters to be dropped into a hole drilled hundreds of feet deep.

Final hookup is made before detonation (right).

The water truck is a vital element of every-day life, its contents pure but rarely even cool, except perhaps in the early morning

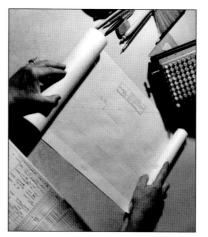

Developing, processing, and interpreting the data captured on the seismic logs is carried out by Tom Garvey, a member of Geophysical Services International (GSI). This office trailer is air conditioned.

The Bedouin delivers the young camel, which is duly inspected and approved by the cook, and, paid off, goes on his way. The camel, admired by Americans and Saudis for a few minutes, is slaughtered on the spot.

The following morning, visitors prepare to board the DC-3, the milkrun for Dhahran.

T. F. Walters

Tents are set at another site several hundred kilos away, for unit SD-1 (structure drill party).

T. F. Walters

Radio aerial goes up promptly as daily communication with Dhahran is crucial.

Checking the aerial before setting out on a morning survey of surrounding area.

Bill Brown lugs tripod, mapping table, and alidade.

T. F. Walters

T. F. Walters

Good food brings contented people. Here, from left, are Harold Smith, Bill Brown, Elmer Hoffman, unknown, and Forrest Cathy.

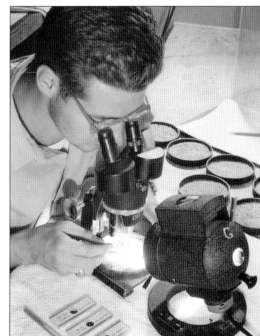

T. F. Walters

Brown classifies samples collected during the day.

Incident at Ras Al Mishaab

They were rare, but incidents of various types—sad, humorous, ludicrous, mysterious—were expected, occurred, and handled quickly and discretely. To survive them, it was important to maintain a sense of equilibrium.

Something had happened at Ras Al Mishaab. Something that required me to head for Aramco's aviation department at Dhahran Airport where a single-engined Navion plane was waiting. The pilot was getting instructions from the dispatcher as I entered the office.

"Take this guy up to Mishaab. Stick around until he does whatever he's supposed to. Don't come back without him," the dispatcher said.

I said, "What's up?"

"I don't know any more than what I just told him," the dispatcher said. "You'll find out when you get up there, I guess," he said. The pilot and I headed out to the aircraft.

Within minutes we were aloft, heading north following the coastline, tan desert on one side, blue water on the other. Flying time was figured at a an hour or so, our ETA shortly before noon. We were at about 3,500 feet, the weather perfect, the outside temperature cool at that height. The Navion was noisier than I had expected. We flew on in silence.

Mishaab was about 150 miles due north of Dhahran, right on the shore, a few miles south of Kuweit. It was the great marshaling yard for the 30–31-inch oil pipeline that

was begun in 1948 and completed in 1950.

As far as I knew, Mishaab was pretty much closed down, except for some maintenance and other calls on the few people still there. It was remote, with access to beaches, fishing, and sailing in the blue Arabian Sea, just enough diversions to maintain a reasonable level of equilibrium.

The plane began to drift down toward some large silvery buildings that glittered in the midday sun, the cockpit getting warmer as we lost elevation. The airfield took on an elongated, rectangular shape. We turned into the wind, the wheels went down and the aircraft floated on to the desert floor. A car waited a short distance away, two men leaning on it. An old Jeep, a Saudi police officer inside, was close by.

Site of the incident.

Once introductions were over, I climbed into the back seat of the sedan, the pilot opting to stay with his plane. We drove off, heading for one of the buildings, the Jeep leading the way. I asked the inevitable question.

"What have you got for me?"

"We'll show you," was the answer. With that, we pulled into a junkyard full of equipment. One of the men pointed to an area next to a small tractor with a boom attached.

"There," he said, pointing to the floor. "Can you get that?"

I was looking at a set of footprints outlined on the floor, then a series of arrows which led to the tractor and disappeared behind it. They were easy to see.

"That's it?" I said.

"That's it," was the answer.

"Well," I said, "I could use a small ladder."

One of the men went off and returned with a stepladder. I climbed up a couple of steps, framed the picture, and made three exposures.

On the way back to the plane, I posed the same question as before. "So, what can you tell me," I said, staring at the backs of the heads of the two guys in front.

"Not much," the driver said. The other one said nothing.

The car pulled up to the Navion, the pilot leaning against it, arms folded.

"Done?" he said.

By late afternoon we were back in Dhahran. I developed the film, provided the security department with prints and a negative, then went home. Nothing was ever said about this incident. Equilibrium was maintained.

KLM Ph-TDL

The Groningen.

The crane and rigging department in Dhahran got a distress call early one morning in late 1954. A KLM Royal Dutch Airline's DC-4 had carried out an emergency landing in the desert about 15 miles north of Dhahran. The pilot had brought the large, four-engined aircraft down successfully among low sand dunes.

Apparently it had a soft landing, sliding through the dunes wheels up, hissing along on its silver belly, sand penetrating every orifice in the lower part of the aircraft as it slowly came to a halt. The props of the radial engines were slightly bent.

There were no injuries to crew or passengers, who were all Moslems on the way to Jiddah, the first leg of the journey to Mecca and Medina. Soon KLM personnel were on the site with doctors and nurses. Busses whisked the passengers to Dhahran Airport and onto another aircraft for Jiddah. It was a miraculous delivery from what could have been a horrific disaster.

With the sun up, officials of KLM and Aramco met. It appears that KLM engineers were on their way from Holland to devise a plan that would get the aircraft up, out of the desert, and back to the airport. It was assumed that men and equipment from Aramco's crane and rigging department would be involved in this tricky task.

The strange apparition that sat down some way off from the downed KLM DC-4 was a helicopter, which flew in from Dhahran Airfield. The property of the United States Air Force, it was the only aircraft that could land and take off from the site, regardless of how weird it looked.

The KLM engineers felt the best way to raise the aircraft was to place a number of large rubber balloons beneath the aircraft, slowly inflate them, and raise the aircraft to the point where the undercarriage could be lowered, examined, and corrected.

It wasn't to be. The balloons could not be stabilized in the sand, without danger of the aircraft tipping over. And there was some concern that the feathered props could not be straightened out onsite. The final judgement was to bring in as many large cranes as were necessary to lift the aircraft, load in onto the biggest trailer Aramco had in the field, and haul it over the desert—very slowly and very carefully—to the highway and home.

Dean Cantrell, a member of the crew, recalls that Chuck Mead, the foreman, calculated that three cranes would be needed to provide "three picking points" to simultaneously elevate the aircraft. About 25 men—crane operators and riggers—would be needed. They figured it would take about a week to do the job.

Everything went as planned as the Americans, Dutchmen, and Saudis toiled away under a blistering sun for six days. On the seventh, the aircraft was set in place on a huge house moving trailer (used by Aramco for moving barastis where needed) and locked down. The only dangerous moment was inching down the slipface of a small dune. That accomplished, the aircraft paused for a moment on a long, level stretch of gravel plain, then headed for Dhahran Airport, with Dean Cantrell at the wheel. Several days later the Groningen departed for Schipol Airport, Amsterdam, Holland.

An unusual challenge, nicely handled.

The aircraft was lifted just high enough to drop and test the undercarriage. All went well.

Steel cable was positioned at the cockpit area of the aircraft.

Chuck Mead checked wheel positions before giving order to the three crane operators to slowly lower the aircraft onto the rig.

With the plane now suspended in mid-air, riggers equalized wheel positions before final placement.

K.R. Webster (white shirt), district manager, confers with Chuck Mead (silver hard hat) and KLM representatives on decision to roll.

The DC-4, delicately balanced on the rig, stayed in place as it slowly came down the face of a small dune.

Dean Cantrell, at the wheel of the Kenworth, waits for the signal to begin the slow journey to the airport. In the background, the last of the cranes heads for Dhahran.

AUB: The Gamble

It was the irony of all ironies.

From the very beginning, the education of its people was a major objective of the Saudi government, clearly stated in the concession agreement and diligently pursued. Aramco was constantly urged to train its employees so that one day they would be skilled enough to run the oil company.

At the same time, it was crucial for Aramco to keep in mind that while it had been permitted to enter the kingdom in search of oil, it had been warned by king and clerics that none of the corrupting aspects of the Western world would be permitted for fear of tainting its people, threatening the religious purity of the nation, the home of Islam. It was an edict that Aramco was constantly reminded of—and to which it placed extremely close attention from day one of its arrival in Saudi Arabia.

But in the early fifties, a serious challenge confronted the Saudi government. The absence of any religious and secular institutions of higher learning in Saudi Arabia capable of further educating qualified young men to become engineers, geologists, scientists, administrators, managers, and executives, would require that they be permitted to continue their education outside of the kingdom. Such a step would expose these young minds to some degree to the corrupting influences of the Western world the government so abhorred. Could these young men withstand the temptations of all kinds and focus their energies and intellects on earning a BA, MA or PhD degree in whatever field they had selected to

It all looks pretty good to this young man. All he has to do is crack the books.

pursue? The irony of it all was inescapable to all familiar with the issue.

Clearly Aramco had done its part, recognizing that the government required it make every effort to train in any way possible the human resources of the nation so that eventually, one day, Saudis would be capable of running the oil operations without benefit of any Americans or for that matter, any foreigners. Just how long it would take—if, indeed it were even possible—was an impenetrable question. Given the undeniable fact that most of the people available to Aramco were still living in a medieval, tenth-century time warp—largely of their own choosing—the task initially defied description, let alone definition and resolution.

It called for Bedouin straight off the desert to train as mechanics and truck drivers. To develop the muscles to become roustabouts on oil rigs, to learn to read construction drawings, to attend daily classes in reading and writing—all tasks assigned to the oil company.

And over time, it did happen, all or most of it.

To an extraordinary degree, Aramco succeeded in evaluating the intellectual capability, the mechanical aptitudes, even the nascent managerial talents spirit of a Bedouin, that village merchant (or probably his son), or more likely a member of the wafer-thin middle class whose children may have traveled with their father outside the kingdom, and were subsequently energized by glimpses of the outside world—and thereby grasped the possibility of a vast life beyond their town, their village, or even their country.

Generation upon generation of Saudis did become engaged in this extraordinary enterprise, carried out over the last 75 years with a degree of success that was thought impossible. There were challenges that would not go away. In those early days there were no colleges and universities within the borders of Saudi Arabia available to talented or promising students who had exhausted the levels of instruction available through Aramco.

It was the classic Catch-22 quandary, a conundrum that perplexed both government officials and clerics alike, although it was eventually resolved in favor of permitting selected students to attend a number of institutions in the Middle East. (Designing and building its own colleges and universities became a priority —the University of Petroleum and Minerals at Dhahran a perfect example of the commitment of the government.)

One of the first colleges selected was the American University of Beirut, usually referred to as the AUB. It was founded in 1866, its original name the Syrian Protestant College through a charter issued in the State of New York. It was located on 73 acres in Beirut, Lebanon, on a hill overlooking the Mediterranean. A beautiful campus, with large handsome buildings, it was within walking distance of downtown Beirut. Then and now, it was considered an outstanding example of the institutions created and financed by Chris-

All six of the young Saudi freshmen take their first stroll around campus.

tian missionaries in the 19th century whose stated goal was to bring education to the Middle East. The distinguished faculty was broad and diversified, including American, British, and Middle Eastern academicians. Today it houses the Schools of Medicine, Science, Engineering and Architecture, and the Suliman Olayan School of Business, offering many degree programs.

Lebanon, of course, was once part of the Ottoman Empire, dismantled following the Armistice that concluded the Great War (1914–1918), and the Sykes-Picot Agreement of 1916, an early effort of the victors (to be) to pick over the best part of the Turkish possessions. The 1921 Peace Treaty held in Paris created a mandate comprised of Lebanon and Syria, to be administrated by France. (Shortly thereafter, following an abortive revolt, Syria was established as a separate entity, still run by the French.)

Beirut was the capital of Lebanon, which even today reflects the culture and character of France. Its natural attributes include a balmy climate along the coast with beautiful beaches and handsome apartments flanking the Rue Corniche. Further inland is the rich Beka Valley with snow in the Anti-Lebanon Mountains for skiing. No wonder Lebanon was often compared with Switzerland, with some reservations.

But Beirut was much more. It was the hub of banking, finance, and business for the Middle East. It was also a major publishing center for all types of books on art, history, architecture, literature, poetry, and languages. The several daily newspapers, published in English, French, and Arabic, were reputed to have the greatest editorial freedom of any such publications in the Middle East. There were cinemas, art galleries, bookstores, bazaars, souks, coffee-houses, restaurants, and nightclubs. Beirut was a sophisticated, cultural oasis offering almost limitless choices for the taking.

There were several fine hotels, such as the St. George, which catered to Americans and Europeans. The Bristol, as the name suggests, largely served the British. The Phoenicia was popular with Middle Easterners. As for the Normandy, all sorts went there, perhaps attracted by the exotic environment created by a night club (the KitKat Club) that featured belly dancers of all types and sizes. Many Aramcons spent at least one of their two-week local leaves in Lebanon, before discovering Nicosia, Cyprus, or London, Paris, or Rome.

Even more astonishing was the government of Lebanon, which was so structured as to acknowledge the religious diversity of the country—Druze, Moslem, and Christian Maronites. Free enterprise was clearly in evidence and the government seemed almost benign in its administration. To use an American colloquial term, it was almost a wide open city, perceived by some as a modern-day Sodom and Gomorroh.

No wonder Riyadh was a bit apprehensive, if not downright alarmed, at determining Beirut as the academic setting for their young, clever, highly impressionable young men to spend four years away from home. No doubt, the process of selecting suitable students had to be carefully carried out to eliminate or reduce to the minimum any embarrassment that might reflect on the Saudi government and nation.

However, at some point—and apparently with no viable alternatives—it was decided that a half dozen young Saudi students attending a college outside the kingdom would make a good story, not only testifying to the ability of the young men to enter a first-class university, but carrying with them the confidence of their government that they would serve as ambassadors of their nation. William Scott, an American who was an instructor in the English department, and who also served as student advisor to the student publications, was invited by Aramco to write an article about one

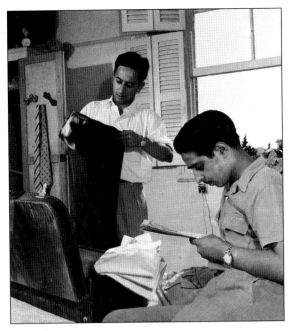

Unpacking.

Meeting.

From almost any view, the campus of AUB is spectacular. Here can be seen the tennis courts, faculty offices, and classrooms. That's the Mediterranean in the distance.

Swimming.

of the first groups of Saudis to attend AUB.

Apparently, it went well.

The six young men were in their early twenties, just a little older than the normal freshmen under-graduates entering college. Smiling, animated, they were obviously pleased to be on campus. They were in western dress—slacks, several with casual sport shirts, a couple with ties. Most wore sports jackets. All spoke English quite well.

O ver the next two days they were photographed settling in at AUB. Unpacking in their rooms, eating at a cafeteria, strolling about the campus. They went swimming one morning, visited the AUB Alumni Club later on, and watched a couple of young women playing tennis on the courts there. Classes would not start until the following week, but they were looking forward to that, all agreed. A little nervously, though.

The next four years were clearly going to be exciting, demand-ing ones for them. This totally new environment, vastly different

from anything they had ever experienced before, was going to fully test their resources. They were going to have to study hard, establish relationships with faculty members, perhaps consider getting involved in campus activities, and begin to make new friends among the student body. As AUB was coeducational, that aspect of campus life might well make life even more intriguing, even exhilarating.

Just how much the distractions offered by downtown Beirut would impinge on these young men was impossible to calculate. As the city was so close to hand, it would be hard to ignore. Anyway, discovery was a large part of the learning process.

I n late 1959, a brief news item in a paper noted that several Saudis had recently graduated from the American University of Beirut. It would have been interesting to learn how many had made the Dean's List. Had any flunked out? Or had any been caught trying to smuggle his girl friend into the dorm? Did a campus romance flourish to the point of marriage? How many had succumbed to any of the vices that their government and religious leaders sought to deny them?

Were their four years a great, exciting time for them?

Inevitably, their horizons must have expanded im-mensely, their options multiplied exponentially, their minds stretching to accommodate, accept—or reject —the vast amounts of new information, new ideas and influences that an open, dynamic society such as Beirut would offer. Freedom was heady stuff. Dan-gerous, too.

Presumably upon graduation, they returned home to Arabia to rejoin Aramco or go into service with the Saudi government, which also needed every young man available to fill the many posts opening up in its many new and expanding departments.

If there is one regret, it might be that a few of them might have sensed the entrepreneurial role that could

be played in serving Saudi Arabia better, knowing what they now knew after exposure to the outside world. But they knew that they were returning to a society still full of strictures that could deny them that opportunity, at least at the very beginning. Now realists more than ever before, they knew their first obligation was to the Saudi government, which had paid for that education.

Hopefully, the gamble paid off—for everybody.

Portraits: The Saudi

In the late forties and early fifties, the gulf that separated the American culture from that of the Saudi was so broad that few people imagined much progress could be made in building the bridges vital to establishing a modern petroleum industry in the country, which concurrently had to be matched by a modern society essential to operating it. Some said it wasn't a gulf, but more like a chasm. They were wrong.

All it took was time. A lot of it. About 75 years, give or take a couple.

Aramco confronted three distinct categories of people it had to work with: 1) the Saudi government, a small cadre in a rarefied environment open to very few outsiders, 2) the retail merchants and small businessmen of the larger towns and villages who represented the razor-thin, but burgeoning middle class, who from their suqs and open-air markets were eager to fill the growing numbers —and needs—of the Americans arriving weekly in Al Hasa Province, and 3) the Bedouin, remote from, and disdainful of the life of the villager and town folk, yet who counted on the merchants to provide the essentials they needed to sustain life, usually bartering their own homemade products to pay for them. They came to town, conducted their business and gladly returned to the desert. Little did they realize that for a good number of them, their lives would be changed forever.

From these disparate elements, Aramco had to establish cordial and productive working relationships with existing (and potential) leaders at various levels of the government; from among its early employees, it had to identify leaders or embryonic managers who could grasp the fundamentals of an industry: its organization, disciplines, objectives, and goals, a near-Herculean task. Finally, people with inherent natural skills (as yet unknown, unmeasured, indeed with no measuring techniques or tools yet in existence) had to be discovered in order to build a workforce of thousands that would be required to carry out the hundreds upon hundreds of specific tasks called for in the running of an oil company. All with the oft-stated objective of replacing every American currently employed in Dhahran, Ras Tanura, Abqaiq—everywhere. And as soon as possible, it was pressed upon Aramco.

A Saudi technician with a career in the oil industry.

Beyond these almost insuperable tasks, Aramco had to look to the future for a new type of person, one who could imagine a business dynamic or generate a vitality far beyond the limited scope of the suq or market-place. It wanted entrepreneurs. Of every and any type who could prevail over geography, temperature, even religion (without ever forgetting what they were). It needed people who knew how to put money to new and different uses, even if they did not have much of it. That was always available to the imaginative, the adventurous, the deserving, it would appear.

And, indeed, a good number showed up, with many of them willing to put together their own talents to meet Aramco's specific needs. In that process, many created unique bonds that over the years have done much to fuel diversity and growth in numerous businesses, which also serve the nation and its people throughout the Kingdom. From tiny acorns…

They had such names as Gosaibi, Ali-Reza, Tamimi, Fouad, and Suliman Olayan. People, families, and groups, they were nothing less than the pioneers of the country. A few were already established, many were brand spanking new. A few failed, but it was not for lack of trying on Aramco's part. In time, the viable operations underwent enormous expansion, yet were themselves often dwarfed by the entry of other players from the Middle East, Europe, and America, aided and abetted by relations formed with princes and others of the royal family. America and the rest of the world queued up in Riyadh, seeking customers and business agents. It was the beginning of the age of infrastructure for a new nation that dealt in cash, not credit.

The pictures on the following pages show but a fragment of the beginning stages of the new vitality and vision that gripped the nation.

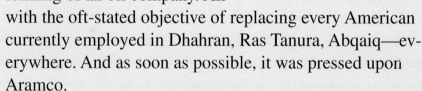

This is General Camp, where most of Aramco's Saudis lived during the week, returning to their homes and families on their day off (usually Friday). A large mosque is centered in the camp. An oil rig still stands on the Dammam Dome, where oil in commercial quantities was finally discovered more than 60 years ago.

A smaller mosque also sits within the camp.

Billiards or pool proved popular.

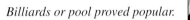

Football (soccer) is a key sport for all ages.

A local police officer daily patrols the the port of Dammam.

A dhow sets out for somewhere with a full load of passengers, as plenty of spectators look on, no doubt some of them wishing they were on board.

Market day in Hofuf is for villagers and Aramco visitors alike.

The larger merchants imported more and better products to meet the growing numbers of women (married and single) eager to decorate their new homes or apartments on arrival in Arabia. Not too much haggling went on.

Pearl divers at Damman dockside.

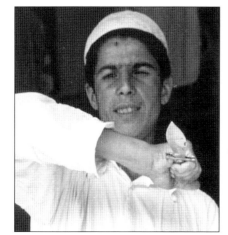

A seller of knives and daggers urged the customer to buy. He did so.

Coffee pots of almost any size and birds of any color are offered by small merchants in most of the suqs.

A day of shopping in Hoffuf, sometimes via the sleek, air-conditioned Budd cars of the SAGRR.

Bud and Liz Ashfield of Dhahran look over a sporty, neat green MG in Al Khobar, which could be shipped from the factory to any destination desired in the world.

A Saudi sales clerk wonders if this young lad is going to buy—or is just "shoofing" the comic book.

Being issued a pair of safety boots is one of the first important acts for a new worker.

Whatever the task, it's important to see eye to eye.

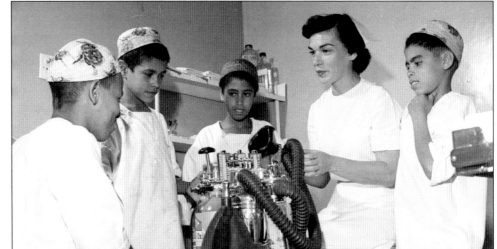

The beginning of instruction for some very young hospital trainee-orderlies, by a nurse at Dhahran Medical Center.

A trainee key-punch operator, on the cusp of the computer world.

Testing every one, a crucial step at Aramco.

The first Saudi team to bring in an oil- well ('54, Shedgum).

Teamwork, a novelty for some, essential for all.

Aramco's air fleet needs lots of helpers.

From the desert, this man can now handle a new task—and grin about it, too.

Once a camel herder, now a bulldozer operator.

Killing the mosquito, ending malaria, was a prime goal of Aramco's medical teams. It was achieved.

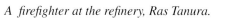

A firefighter at the refinery, Ras Tanura.

Saudi worker at tank farm.

Sometimes you just have to shout.

Collection point at Sidon, Lebanon.

At the very beginning.

Brute strength, stamina, speed, coordination, all needed to make good roustabouts.

A trio of trainmen, hauling product.

Bulkplant handling gasoline, kerosene, other oil products.

Running a gas station.

Then the three R's.

That lead to entry level jobs.

Trying to capture a sense of the physical scale, enormity and complexity of the first major industry to be created in Saudi Arabia was daunting for many, including many Americans.

On-the-job training was a crucial element in the educational process, where the Saudi who demonstrated an interest coupled with aptitude, was assured of encouragement and rewards. Here, Ash Kearney, of the producing department, with a promising candidate.

The task is to get the product from Safaniya or the Shedgum to ships waiting offshore at Sidon.

Better paying, cleaner jobs (even air-conditioned offices!) are for those who can see the opportunities that are often right in front of them.

99

Joe Flom.

Visitors

Once the Western world had acknowledged that the discovery of oil in Saudi Arabia might make it a major player in the energy field, all sorts of people wanted to see for themselves.

Visitors began to line up at the gates to Saudi Arabia, either at Jiddah, the traditional point of entry on the west coast, or the new point of entry, Dhahran, in Al Hasa Province. Some people had been invited and duly entered the country to meet government and oil industry officials; others who had invited themselves waited, sometimes failing to win the approval of the government. Aramco was eventually invited to manage this function. (See "Keeper of the Gates", page 26.)

They were of every imaginable type. Various kings, lesser potentates, many business men, plus a few commoners— and the new adventurers: writers, editors, journalists, and photographers of all stripes. Executives from the parent companies of Aramco came to look over the operations of their latest investment.

Business men preferred to travel incognito. For those powerful enough to travel in their own aircraft, and interested in meeting privately with the government, Dhahran was bypassed for a direct approach to Riyadh—once approval to land had been secured. They came and went unnoticed, undocumented by camera.

Rumors spoke of mysterious flights and exotic people coming and going. Could that really have been Aristotle Onassis? Was that private jet carrying one of the Rock-

Adelai L. Stevenson, who just lost his bid for the presidency, visits Saudi Arabia and Aramco.

efellers (David, probably)? Perhaps J. Paul Getty, one of the world's most successful—and mysterious—oil moguls. Or Kim Philby, Middle East correspondent for

the London Daily Telegraph, on a visit to his father, H. St. John B. Philby. For those who sought privacy, more often than not they received it. Aramco surely got a little nervous when some of these heavy hitters came into town (Riyadh, not Dhahran) for its concession agreement was a precious, fragile document that always seemed to be undergoing some review or proposed modification in Riyadh or Jiddah.

For members of the fourth estate, the rules were simple: if the Saudi government felt that the kingdom would be treated fairly, enter. To name a few visitors: Wells Hangen of the the New York Times, Harry F. Ellis, Christian Science Monitor, Joe Flom, U.S. News & World Report, Wanda Jablonski, Journal of Commerce, Sam Souki and Harry Kern, Newsweek, Robert Hewitt, Associated Press, Keith Wheeler of Time, and local journalists from Lebanon and Syria, such as Joseph Sidke, Al Jaridah, and Clovis Ridk, L'Orient.

One of the most aggressive—and, therefore most successful—still photographers was David Douglas Duncan, who secured scoops by simply flying into Riyadh or Jiddah and endearing himself to various officials, the results showing up in Life magazine. Chutzpah comes to mind.

If an article upon publication was thought to be too critical of the government, that issue might arrive at Aramco's commissaries with that specific piece scissored out. The next time that wayward journalist might not find it so easy to secure an exist visa, which is far more important than an entry permit.

(left) U.S. military and State Department guests are welcomed by honor guards at Dhahran Airport.

The Republican victory in 1952 put Dwight D. Eisenhower in the White House, just as the Cold War was heating up. The administration began to pay more attention to events in the Middle East and their implications for America, as the creation of Israel further complicated the political arena.

John Foster Dulles, new secretary of state, accompanied by Harold Stassen, a presidential advisor, came to see for themselves the countries and the people they would be working with for the next four years. The problems would be many and complex, very few of them subject to easy resolution. Invariably, they were linked to the Middle East, it bubbling away with such developments as a new king of Jordan, turmoil in Egypt, with the oil industry a backdrop to many of these happenings.

Harry F. Ellis was the Middle East correspondent for the Christian Science Monitor for many years. Based in Beirut, he visited Arabia frequently, endearing himself to Aramco and the Saudi government for his fair, even-handed treatment of the complex issues of the area and era.

Generals come and go; on inspection trips to U.S. airbase at Dhahran.

Mr. Fred Davies and Mr. Floyd Ohliger, both in whites, and their guests Dulles and Stassen, seem to be in very good spirits as they emerge from Aramco's administration building in Dhahran.

These B-29s seemed to be permanent visitors at Dhahran Air Field.

Shaikh of Bahrain, right, is met at airport by King Sa'ud.

U.S. sailors based in Bahrain arrive by launch, accompanied by the shore patrol.

King Hussein of Jordan visited King Sa'ud in Dammam, the first time they had met as new monarchs of their respective countries. As such, they had much to talk about, fences to mend, and new alliances to consider. Egypt was in turmoil, for Gamel Abdul Nasser had seized power there, setting in motion a series of events that would change the Middle East landscape for ever. The recent death of Stalin and the emergence of Khrushchev further complicated the world politician situation.

H. St. John B. Philby was a frequent guest of Aramco. He spoke before its management about all sorts of Middle East topics, including his impressions about the Saudi government and its shortcomings. Such comments caused considerable friction in Riyadh, but Philby was unrelenting and he was eventually banned from the country in 1955.

Middle East publishers showed up regularly.

Lowell Thomas, Jr., a world traveler much like his father, visited him during the shooting of a feature produced by Cinerama. He and his wife Charlie flew their single-engined plane into Dhahran, on their way to Aden.

Cinerama, which chartered its own plane to haul the thousands of pounds of equipment needed, was an unusual visitor that showed up one day at Hofuf Airfield.

Hollywood came to Hofuf in the person of John Farrow, a well-known motion-picture director who directed sequences of the film produced by Cinerama. He was married at one point to Maureen O'Sullivan, a famous film star (she was Tarzan's girlfriend, among other roles). They were the parents of Mia Farrow of Rosemary's Baby fame.

Ambassador George Wadsworth takes a minute away from diplomacy for an equally tough challenge—golf at Rolling Hills Golf Club, Dhahran.

A concert pianist on tour in the Middle East was prevailed upon to add Dhahran to his itinerary, to the enjoyment of almost everyone.

Members of the royal family, on a visit to Dhahran, pausing for a moment at Executive House for this picture.

Alfred W. Lilienthal was a surprise visitor to Dhahran in September of 1954. An American Jew, he had written a book, What Price Israel, which challenged the need for the creation of the state of Israel on political, moral, and religious grounds. Published in 1953, it brought him invitations to speak at many forums, including Dhahran, Riyadh, and Israel.

The captain of the first supertanker, the S.S. Seria Maru, to take on product at Ras Tanura.

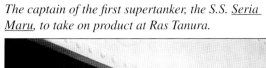

The gentleman shaking hands with King Sa'ud is the father of Fred A. Davies, president and CEO of Aramco. Mr. Davies was spending a few days with his son, staying at the Max Steineke guest house in Dhahran.

Dick Lyford was a frequent visitor over many years, producing numerous health-medicine related films, even a major feature production.

A young Aramcon gets a friendly pat on the head and a smile from King Sa'ud, as Fred A. Davies stands by.

Qata!

Qata!

The Qata is like a sand grouse, somewhat like a partridge in coloration, appearance, and flight. It serves the Bedouin well as a food source, particularly those with a good shotgun and keen eyesight.

On the flat hard gravel plains between the red sand dunes of the Dahanas and the marshy sabahah that lay before the capital city Riyadh, these birds can often be found. The bird does not seem to understand what a shotgun blast signifies, or the crumpled bodies of its fellows.

Some time ago, while traveling with a reconnaissance crew of the exploration department that was in the area south of the Al Kharj Farm, we came upon a host of these small birds.

Don Bogle, right, with Sam Roach next to him, and the men who accompanied them. This picture is taken near Air Dar.

They came into view as a brownish, swirling smudge in the sky as we were speeding across a shimmering gravel plain, a dark mass of sweeping, diving shapes about a mile ahead and to the right of our position. The driver, Don Bogle, a geologist, kept his eye on them, twisted the steering wheel and headed in their direction. In a couple of minutes we could clearly see the birds hovering in the sky, coming closer and closer to the ground. They finally settled down on the plain, now about a hundred yards

from us. There might have been a couple of hundred of them, seemingly unaware of us approaching. Bogle stopped the car and we stared at them for several minutes, silent in the intense mid-day heat.

Finally, Bogle instructed me to load the 12-gauge shotgun, shove it out the window, and wait. He then proceeded to drive in a large circle around the birds who, irritated, skittered toward the center of it. Bogle made another circle, this time tighter. Yet another circle, tighter still. He made another, and finally stopped the car about 20 yards from the jostling birds. They made a tight brown patch on the light desert plain. Not one had taken to the air.

I turned to Sam Harper, chief of the party, and said, "O.K., who's going to holler at them?"

"Hell," said Sam. "You don't holler at 'em, just shoot 'em where they sit!"

I slid back the safety, aimed at the center of the brown mass of the birds and slowly squeezed the trigger. The blast brought the living Qata up and away, swirling across the desert, leaving about a dozen still and fluttering shapes dotted on the gravel floor.

In the distance we saw the mass of birds circling slowly, coming closer and closer to the earth again. Finally, they sat down.

We got out of the car and collected all of the birds and put them in a sack used to collect samples of rocks and shale. It got a bit bloody but the sack was woven tightly. Eleven birds in all, they were thrown in the trunk.

Once back in the car, Bogle hit the gas pedal and we went speeding across the plain after the birds. About a hundred yards from them, Bogle again began his circling movements, again and again until the birds were in a tight bunch, little more than 25 yards from our car. This was the moment when I decided that they were a little careless, if not stupid.

We stopped. This time Bogle fired. Again the birds flew off, this time barely brushing the gravel for a long time before rising intro the sky and breaking off to the right of

---

(left) The oryx is rarely seen in the desert these days. These baker's dozen or so were bred in captivity near Riyadh.

us. We collected another dozen or so birds, put them in the sack, now nearly full, and headed off in the direction of Al Kharj. Our hunt was over.

As we approached a sand dune area directly in our path, we talked about the lack of sportsmanship just demonstrated by all of us. No one could understand the suicidal behavior of the birds. It wasn't as if they were unfamiliar with the sound of firearms. Most Bedouins used some type of shotgun, although they often hunted with falcons. It was a mystery. Our biggest problem was what to do with the birds.

In the midst of the dunes and traveling at the top speed possible to avoid getting trapped in the treacherous soft sand, we ground our way around and in between steep dunes that seemed to have slip faces as sharp as razors. All of a sudden we came upon a small camel train, about a dozen or so of them laden with firewood, accompanied by four Bedouin. They saw us, waved and beckoned to us to stop.

We stopped. We always did, soft sand or not, although we drove within a few yards of the camels and picked what we all hoped was a firm stretch of sand. The leader of the foursome, a lean, weathered fellow, came up to us, peered into the car, went through the pattern of greeting us, each in turn, then finally said, "Miyah" (water)? We unhooked one of the desert water bags carried outside the car and gave it to him. He upended it but drank sparingly. The others took their turn. We also filled a small aluminum container one of the men brought to the car. We were glad to be of help to them.

Then for a few moments we talked. It was relatively easy to do. Customary greetings are long and elaborate in Arabia. Both Bogle and Harper had the process down pretty well. It is a pattern that can be most enjoyable to both parties, if offered with sincerity and spirit. When asked where we were going, they all said that Al Kharj was very beautiful. We agreed.

About this point, Sam asked them if they would like some birds we had just shot. He got out, opened the trunk, then the sack, and dumped all the birds out on the sand. At this the men shouted with pleasure at seeing so many. One man picked up a bird and thrust the head and neck in his mouth, grinning as he did so.

"Al Hum Dililah!" he sang out.

They took them all, wrapped the birds in a colored piece of cloth and threw the bundle across the lead camel. We said goodbye, shook hands, climbed back into the car, got traction right away, and headed for the farm.

The economics of it all made sense. For the cost of a few 12-gauge shotgun shells, we had gained about two dozen birds, enough meat for a couple of good meals for the Bedouin. Something good had come out of our hunt for Hubara.

It was time for a cup of ghawar, a steaming hot cup of coffee in the blistering sun that, strongly flavoured with cardamon, was strangely refreshing, even cooling.

We came upon a great hole in the desert, set against the backdrop of a massive escarpment.

Slowly churning our way through a series of low dunes, we came upon a number of camels grazing all by themselves, it seemed. But shortly thereafter, we found their owners.

A little pistol and revolver practice during the day.

PROD. *ISLAND OF ALLAH*

SCENE	TAKE
180	1

Roll

On Making Movies

In Hollywood, Hofuf, or Riyadh…

It's always the same. Hurry up and wait.

Six men have just returned from a trip to the capital, Riyadh. It was a physically and emotionally exhausting experience, although very little work was done, manual or mental. But working with palace counselors, princes, and the king of Arabia can at times be downright debilitating, almost nerve-wracking. The isolation that a large, dark gloomy—though cool, thank heavens—and very quiet palace engenders, can also add to the feeling that, perhaps, somebody has forgotten all about you.

The objective of this visit was to shoot a simple, brief movie sequence of King Sa'ud. It would complete a documentary film covering the rise of his father, Sa'ud Ibn Abdul Aziz Al Sa'ud, the consolidation of the country by him, the discovery of oil, and the bright future of the country that was beginning to unfold.

This film sequence—or insert—was expected to run in its final, edited form no longer that 30 seconds, a somewhat static shot with the king seated at a desk in his office in the new Nasiriyah Palace. The movie, eventually called Jazirat al Arab, was being made by Dick Lyford Productions, an independent film company. Recruited by Aramco, the company had already produced several short educational films on preventive medicine, the conservation of water, the eradication of the fly, and other subjects. All of them had been well-received by Aramco and the government.

Jazirat Al Arab, however, was conceived as a more ambitious 'feature film.' Although much of the footage would be shot in Saudi Arabia, the historical scope of the film would require the film crew to cover parts of Europe, the Middle East, and Asia and reflect the reach and impact of Islam from the 7th century on, concluding at about the 14th century. The consolidation of Arabia by Ibn Sa'ud

Murabbah Palace, home of the late king, was large, gloomy, dark—but very cool.

and the administration of the new oil kingdom by his heir, Sa'ud, beginning in 1954, would complete the film. It was a major production, no doubt about it, and took all of two years to complete. Naturally, the government

endorsed the concept, approved the script, and largely financed it.

Once completed, the film was expected to be released in the Middle East, where it was expected to enjoy a good reception. It might also be well received in other, selected parts of the world. As for its distribution in the U.S., with a considerably more diverse or complex audience, its acceptability, let alone its success, would be somewhat more difficult to predict.

From the filmmaker's point of view, it was crucial that the present king of Arabia be featured. Thus negotiations with this in mind were conducted several months before the scheduled completion of the film. A rough cut of portions of the film, assembled and screened for him, met his approval and he agreed to be photographed. Once this approval was granted, plans were made to assemble a film crew that could move at a minute's notice to Riyadh, about a two-hour flight due west of the oil company's headquarters at Dhahran.

The film crew was comprised of the producer, Dick Lyford, principal cameraman and an electrical wizard, Pat Patton, who knew all about the power and sound ends of the business; the art director, Eric Mose, who also doubled as an assistant cameraman; Ray T. Graham, for many years a communications consultant to Aramco, who would serve as an observer and grip; Isa Sabbagh, a well-known Middle East radio personality (and interpreter) who ultimately narrated the finished film; and a still photographer, who would shoot stills of the filming of the king. He'd also serve as another grip, responsible for shifting, lifting, and lugging about all sorts of camera gear, as required.

As instructed, we'd stuck close to home and waited for the call, something that we expected would happen quickly, as the anniversary of the king's ascension to the throne was coming up and we did not want that event to complicate or delay our plans. After all, we barely needed an hour to get the footage required to wrap up the entire film. We waited. The days went by slowly, with no word from Riyadh. People in our government relations department attempted to get things moving, to no avail. Nothing but silence from Riyadh. The pilot was on immediate standby, his plane ready to go, all were advised. Please stand by.

First morning, a good breakfast—and ready to go to work.

Late one afternoon, exactly nine days before the coronation anniversary, the call came. The plane would leave at 6 a.m. the following morning for Riyadh. That night, all the equipment: cameras, film, filters, tripods, lights, tape recorders, reflectors, batteries, and a tool kit, were checked. Twice. And then once more. And, even though traveling within the kingdom, it was urged that passports were in hand.

The next morning, picked up and delivered to the airport, a DC-3 was waiting, its engines idling in the coolness of the early morning. Bags and equipment were stacked neatly by the entry door, at

Of cameras and cars, fourth day. Waiting for the call.

which point each piece was examined by a Saudi customs official, presumably checking for contraband before he permitted it to be loaded on the aircraft. Finally, he examined all passports.

Within minutes we were in the air, now cool and pleasant, just a few thousand feet high, which we maintained throughout the entire flight. Below us we could see the largely featureless desert, yielding few shadows, only the different colors of the floor—red, brown, tan, and blinding white. Now and then I spotted some black rectangular spots, tents of Bedouins, and, nearby, a few camels, goats, and sheep. Only when we were an hour or so into our journey did the early morning sun cast longer shadows of a few small jebels or foot hills, numerous dry wadis, and at one point the mighty impressive Tuwaiq Escarpment. But not one single blade of green grass, as far as I could see.

A couple of hours into the flight, the co-pilot walked back and advised us that he had received from Riyadh a radio message that permitted our entry into the capital as guests of the king. This impressed all of us and confirmed our hopes that they were expecting us and that the scene would be shot on schedule. Once in the can the film crew could close down its operations and return to the States to edit the film.

An hour or so later, the pilot came back and said that Riyadh was coming into view, and that we would be on the ground in a half-hour. I had mixed feelings about heading down to the blazing-hot desert floor, as the air temperature at our cruising height of 8,000 feet was pleasant and refreshing. Approaching Riyadh, we began to drift down and turned to line up with the airport runway. We noticed several sleek Convair aircraft lined up on the tarmac, which comprised the new air fleet of the just-formed Saudi Airlines.

Employees going home, everyday.

The waiting game, day six. Glum faces, civility in short supply.

Our landing, soft and predictable, was welcomed by several cars and a couple of station wagons, which sped out to meet us but, misjudging our arrival point, had to follow us as we turned and taxied to the main gate and came to a stop. As we opened the rear door, a blast of hot air hit us. We were greeted by a member of the king's household, an elegant young Saudi. Another good sign. As usual, once the gear was unloaded we checked it on the ground, then loaded it in the two station wagons, the pilot standing by through all this process. When completed, he turned and climbed aboard the DC-3 through the cargo door entrance, pulling the ladder up and inside. As he began to swing the door shut, we hollered at him to learn where he would be later that day, once we'd finished up.

"Hey, I'm leaving now," he said. "My instructions were to bring you here and then head back to Dhahran."

"But this job is only going to take at the most a couple of hours," we wailed. "Stick around," we urged, "the country air will do you good."

"Nothing doing," he answered. We figured that was final. So we were in for an overnight stay and could catch the milk-run flight that came up every morning. As the plane took off, we wondered when we'd see him again.

As we entered the city of Riyadh, our escort informed us that we would be staying at Mubarrah Palace, not Baker Camp, Aramco's facilities at the airport, a surprise to us. Mubarrah was once the principal residence of Ibn Sa'ud, he proudly informed us. The journey through the city was hot, dusty, and bumpy, the street filled with people; our driver maneuvered slowly but still had to honk his way through the throngs.

The interior of Riyadh was intriguing, a maze of narrow streets and tiny alleys, with the crenellated tops of several of the larger buildings trimmed in whitewash. The brown mud walls, topped off with white, and above that a bright blue, cloudless sky, made

Dry run. Lyford (biggest man on team) sits in for King Sa'ud behind desk, as camera is positioned for shot. It is day ten, about 9 p.m. Sabbagh, Patton, and Graham stand by.

The King arrives at 11 p.m., takes position at desk, and accepts a prop from Shaikh Abdullah Bulkhair. Lyford checks meter reading for lights. Shiny walls are problem that can't be solved.

Suddenly, phone on desk rings as filming is about to begin. King Saud, not missing a beat, takes the call, keeps it brief, then hangs up.

Showtime! Graham handles the clapper, the camera rolls, the king is on cue. Action!

Day Eleven. The plane is at the airport. A long time for a crucial bit of film.

for a pleasing architectural image. Here and there we noticed small air conditioning units wedged into windows, a modern incongruous detail. We eventually arrived at Mubarrah, a very large structure, dark reddish in color, ominously quiet, with few people in sight as we pulled into a small courtyard and waited.

Our driver went inside and soon staff and servants spilled out from the interior to help us with our equipment and baggage. Given large bedrooms on the second floor, we were shown the dining room, where we were informed we would have all our meals (as Asa Sabbagh, serving as interpreter, informed us). As a normal course, we checked all of our gear again and waited for the call from Nasiriyah Palace. It was midday and figured that, with a bit of luck, we could get the shot needed that afternoon and call it a wrap. Then we could inform Dhahran and schedule our return for the following morning.

It was not to be, as these pictures show.

أرامكو السعودية

Ray T. Graham.

Aramco Is No More

In the summer of 2002, Ray T. Graham received an invitation to meet Abdallah Jum'ah, president and chief executive officer of Saudi Aramco, at a reception and dinner held on Monday, June 17 at the Roof Terrace Restaurant, the Kennedy Center for the Performing Arts, Washington, D.C.

Ray, curious at receiving the invitation but pleasantly surprised, responded that he would attend. David D. Bosch had been with Aramco since 1973. For several years, he had known Ray and the work he had done as a graphics and communications consultant for Aramco. It was David Bosch who had extended the invitation. Ray, now 89 and long retired, was still in touch with a few of the men and women with whom he had worked over the years.

Actually, the dinner had several objectives. As part of a continuing public information program since the remaining assets of Aramco were purchased by the Saudi Arabian government and the company renamed Saudi Aramco (in 1988), one objective was to inform the public about developments in Saudi Aramco and to emphasize the strong historical ties to the U.S. It also created an opportunity to expose the new, young managers of the company to a wide-ranging review of current industrial, political, economic, and cultural attitudes of America.

About 25 young Saudis of diverse educational disciplines, and holding key positions in the company, had just completed a two-week-long management seminar in Washington. Thus this assemblage of some old friends, some new ones, and future executives of Saudi Aramco,

provided its chief executive officer with an ideal opportunity to talk to them in an intimate, informal social setting.

It all went very well. Ray bumped into a couple of people he knew. He met most of the young Saudi managers and was impressed at their credentials and growing sophistication. Eventually, he was introduced to Abdallah Jum'ah, who asked him about his connection with Aramco. Ray recalls the conversation was along the following lines.

Abdallah Jum'ah (center) with managers of SaudiAramco.

Essam Tewfiq

"Well, it reaches back to the early 1940s," he said. " I was asked to produce in a short period of time a great deal of financial data in simple, graphic presentations to assist CASOC in seeking additional funds to continue drilling in Al Hasa."

Ray recalls that the chief executive officer smiled, and remarked that that was a few years before he was born—but he was certainly pleased to meet the man who

had helped find the money for CASOC. Both of them were now aware that together they had more than a hundred years of knowledge and experience with Aramco and Saudi Arabia. They parted on most cordial terms, closing with the traditional Arabic wish. "Fi Aman Allah (Go in the name of God)."

For Ray it was a fitting way to conclude a remarkable, 60-year association with Aramco and the kingdom of Saudi Arabia.

I am indebted still further to David D. Bosch and Arthur P. Clark for their joint assistance in securing the picture at left taken by Essam Tawfiq, assistant to Abdallah Jum'ah, and reviewing the text as to its appropriateness and accuracy.

Mud bricks make way for...

Bibliography

Arnold, Thomas & Guillaume, Alfred, Editors. <u>The Legacy of Islam</u>, Oxford University Press, 1952. London, England.

Barger, Thomas C. <u>Out In The Blue, Letters from Arabia—1937 to 1940</u>. Selwa Press, 2000. Vista, California.

Butler, Grant C. <u>Kings and Camels</u>. The Devin-Adair Company, 1960. New York.

Cheney, Michael Sheldon. <u>Big Oil Man From Arabia</u>. Ballentine Books, 1958. New York.

Clark, Angela. <u>Bahrein Oil and Development 1929-1989</u>. International Research Center for Energy and Economic Development (ICEED), 1990. University of Colorado, Boulder, Colorado.

Dialdin, Ali M & Tahlawi, Muhammad A, Editors. <u>Saudi Aramco And Its People, A History of Training</u>. Aramco Services Company, 1998.

Field, Michael. <u>From Unayzah to Wall Street, The Story of Suliman Saleh Olayan</u>. John Murray, 2000. London.

Finnie, David H. <u>Desert Enterprise</u>. Harvard University Press, 1958. Cambridge, Massachusetts.

Hourani, Albert. <u>A History of The Arab Peoples</u>. The

Belknap Press of Harvard University Press, 1991. Cambridge, Massachusetts.

Kheirallah, George. <u>Arabia Reborn</u>. The University of New Mexico Press, 1952. Albuquerque, New Mexico.

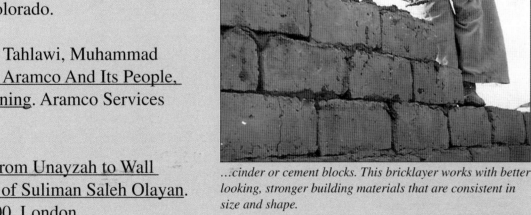

...cinder or cement blocks. This bricklayer works with better looking, stronger building materials that are consistent in size and shape.

Lebkicher, Roy; Rentz, George; & Max Steineke. <u>Aramco Handbook</u>. Arabian American Oil Company, 1960. New York.

MacMillian, Margaret. <u>Paris 1919</u>. Random House, 2001. New York.

McConnell, Philip C. <u>The Hundred Men</u>. Currier Press, 1985. Peterborough, New Hampshire.

Nawwab, Ismail I., Speers, Peter C., & Hoye, Paul F., Editors. <u>Saudi Aramco and Its World: Arabia And The Middle East</u>. The Saudi Arabian Oil Company, 1995. Dhahran, Saudi Arabia.

Philby, H. St. John B. <u>Arabian Jubilee</u>. Robert Hale Limited, 1952. London.

Lilienthal, Alfred M. <u>What Price Israel?</u> Henry Regnery Company, 1953. Chicago, Illinois.

Lippman, Thomas W. <u>Inside The Mirage. America's Fragile Partnership with Saudi Arabia</u>, Westview Press, 2004. Cambridge, Massachusetts.

Sander, Nestor. <u>Ibn Saud: King by Conquest</u>, Hats Off Books, 2001.

Stark, Freya. <u>The Southern Gates of Arabia</u>. John Murray, 1946. London, United Kingdom.

Stark, Freya. <u>Passionate Nomad</u>. The Modern Library, 2001. New York.

Stegner, Wallace. <u>Discovery!</u> Middle East Export Press, 1971. Beirut, Lebanon.

Ward, Thomas E. <u>Negotiations for Oil Concessions in Bahrain, El Hasa (Saudi Arabia), The Neutral Zone, Qatar and Kuwait</u>. Privately printed, 1965. New York.

Other Publications
Saudi Aramco World (bi-monthly)

Al~Ayyam Al~Jamilah (quarterly)
Aramco Service Company, Houston, Texas.

Dimensions (periodical)
Dhahran, Saudi Arabia

New buildings using such new materials can go up faster—and much higher.